THE SECOND ONE THOUSAND YEARS

The Second One Thousand Years

Ten People Who Defined a Millennium

Edited by

RICHARD JOHN NEUHAUS

WILLIAM B. EERDMANS PUBLISHING COMPANY
GRAND RAPIDS, MICHIGAN / CAMBRIDGE, U.K.

© 2001 Wm. B. Eerdmans Publishing Co.
All rights reserved

Wm. B. Eerdmans Publishing Co.
255 Jefferson Ave. S.E., Grand Rapids, Michigan 49503 /
P.O. Box 163, Cambridge CB3 9PU U.K.
www.eerdmans.com

Printed in the United States of America

09 08 07 06 05   10 9 8 7 6 5

Library of Congress Cataloging-in-Publication Data

The second one thousand years: ten people who defined a millennium /
edited by Richard John Neuhaus
p.   cm.
Contents:
Gregory VII and the politics of the spirit / Robert Louis Wilken —
The mind of Maimonides / David Novak —
Thomas Aquinas, a doctor for the ages / Romanus Cessario —
Dante, a party of one / Robert Hollander —
Columbus and The beginning of the world / Robert Royal —
Calvin and the Christian calling / Alister McGrath —
Pascal, the first modern Christian / Edward T. Oakes —
Rousseau and the revolt against reason / Mary Ann Glendon —
Abraham Lincoln and the last best hope / Jean Bethke Elshtain —
John Paul II and the crisis of humanism / George Weigel.
ISBN 0-8028-4905-9 (pbk.: alk. paper)
1. Civilization, Christian.   2. Civilization, Western.
I. Neuhaus, Richard John.

BR115C5.S34   2001
270 — dc21
00-065419

The essays collected in this volume all previously appeared in *First Things: A Monthly Journal of Religion and Public Life.*

Contents

CONTENTS

Introduction

RICHARD JOHN NEUHAUS

IT MIGHT AS WELL BE ADMITTED. The dawning of a new millennium was something of a letdown for most people. More precisely, it was not a letdown because they were never very excited about it in the first place. There is the factor that two-thirds of the world is outside the orbit of what some persist in calling Christian civilization, and the idea of a "third millennium" is undeniably Christian in origin. Just because almost all the world is today compelled to mark time by the Western calendar does not mean that "others" have to invest that way of keeping time with spiritual or cultural significance. In fact, the suggestion that they should do so is frequently resented as an instance of cultural imperialism.

Then, too, there is the pedants' point that the timing is all off. Actually, they have two points. First, Jesus was not born in the Year One but, most likely, in the year we call 6 B.C. By that reckoning, the third millennium began in 1994 or 1995. The second point of pedantry is that the second millennium did not end until the end of the year 2000. The chronological fuzziness about the date undoubtedly contributed to putting a damper on millennial excitements. Moreover, it is not only the two-thirds world that is disinclined to celebrate a date of distinctly Christian significance. Among the bien pesant of the West, there is a widespread, indeed dominant, sense that there is something not quite right about paying public attention to a Christian marking of time. In many cases, this sense is driven by hostility to Christianity; more frequently, I expect, it is based in a taken-for-granted assumption that ours is no longer a Christian civilization. To which some routinely add, "If it ever was."

Within the various Christian communities as well, the dawning of the third millennium occasioned a lukewarm response. The great exception of course was the Catholic Church, which includes somewhat over half the Christians in the world. In 1994 John Paul II issued an apostolic letter, *Tertio Millennio Adveniente* (As the Third Millennium Nears), laying out an ambitious program for the observance of the Jubilee Year 2000. The letter included a strong invitation to other Christian communities, in both the East and the West, to join in the planning and celebration of the Jubilee Year. And there was impressive ecumenical participation in some parts of the program, such as the opening of the great millennial door of St. Peter's in Rome. But, for the most part, the response of other Christian communities to the Pope's invitation was, to put it gently, cool. Perhaps because the planning by Rome was already so far advanced, and others felt they were being asked to sign on to an essentially Catholic observance. In fact, John Paul II had been talking about, anticipating, and planning the Jubilee Year since his election as Bishop of Rome in 1978. His intuition — some would say mystical intuition — that he was elected to lead the Church across the threshold of the third millennium is no secret. An additional discouragement in the ecumenical response was the frostiness of the Orthodox Church, notably the Russian Orthodox, to John Paul II's many initiatives to advance ecclesial reconciliation between East and West.

And so it was that the Jubilee Year was very largely a Catholic affair. At least in terms of programmatic response, the dawning of the third millennium was no big deal for Baptists, Methodists, Lutherans, Presbyterians, and all the other Christian communions. But for many, perhaps most, Catholics, and most especially for John Paul II, it was a very big deal indeed. Almost every day of the year was dedicated to a special millennial observance — for evangelization, for the medical profession, for scientists, for journalists, and on and on. Hundreds of thousands of pilgrims, more than twenty million over the course of the year, came to Rome for these special observances. A physically fragile pope drove himself to personally participate day by day, delivering literally hundreds of homilies and exhortations, presiding over thousands of hours of ceremonies, always exhorting, admonishing, encouraging, and proposing new initiatives. One cardinal was heard to complain, "This pope does not understand that the Church cannot be kept in a state of perpetual agitation."

Amidst the swirl of activities were some events that earned the title "historic." There was, for instance, the commemoration of twentieth-century martyrs, including Catholic, Orthodox, and Protestant heroes and heroines who had died for the faith. The first Sunday of Lent witnessed the Mass of Reconciliation in which the Church confessed the sins of her sons and daughters over the millennium past. This received tremendous attention in the media, being misleadingly depicted as the Church's "apology" to the world. Then there was the pilgrimage to the Holy Land in which, from Sinai to Pentecost, John Paul II "recapitulated" the entire biblical story of salvation. (The pilgrimage was supposed to have started in Ur, where Abraham was first called to be the father of nations, but the Iraqi government placed impossible political conditions on the Pope's visit, so there was a "spiritual pilgrimage" to Ur held at the Vatican.)

But I return to my first point. For most of the world, and for most Christians, the dawning of a new millennium did not occasion much excitement. To be sure, there was considerable excitement, or at least media hype, about the threatening "Y2K Crisis." In the nineteenth century, end-of-the-world scenarios had to do with the return of Christ and the establishment of the Kingdom of God. This time around the anticipated apocalypse was a global computer crash. Some might think it appropriate that, in a world driven by "the technological imperative" (Jacques Ellul), eschatology was reduced to the inability of machines to recognize the digits "00." While some survivalists hoarded food in the wilderness, Y2K turned out to be, as apocalypses go, something of a bust. As a media entertainment, it was a safe excitement, not least because it was untainted by religious significance. Also avoiding anything so "controversial" as religion, never mind Christianity in particular, was the much derided Millennium Dome in London. On the other hand, the U.S. as a nation had no official observance of the millennium at all. Given the confused state of our culture and what kind of official millennial project it might have produced, that is perhaps just as well.

The nineteenth-century journalist Elbert Hubbard is reported to have said, "History is just one damned thing after another." It has become a commonplace to accuse Americans in particular of lacking a sense of history. In this connection, Henry Ford's maxim is regularly trotted out, "History is bunk." Generalizations about the American lack of historical consciousness should, I think, be treated with a measure of skepticism. One must always ask, Compared to whom? Certainly, the Europe of the European Union seems to be set upon inducing a massive seizure of amnesia regarding the national histories, which are inescapably Christian histories, that once defined Europe. But it is true that most close students of American culture have deemed it to be impatient with the past, eager to get on with the enjoyment of the present and the exploration of possibilities as yet unimagined. And, to the extent that is right, it is undoubtedly one reason why people almost everywhere view America, with a mix of admiration and envy, as the lead society of world-historical change. America has "FUTURE" written all over it.

Those who believe in the Lord of history, however, cannot be so dismissive of the past. After all, in the Christian scheme of things, our future has been revealed in the past. That is simply to say that the ultimate past and the ultimate future, the Alpha and Omega, has appeared in time in Jesus the Christ. The lighting of the paschal candle in the Easter Vigil is accompanied by the words, "All time belongs to Christ, and all the ages." This does not mean that history is over. On the cross, Christ declared, "It is finished." It is finished, but it is not over. The great battle has been fought and won, but subsequent history is not anti-climactic; it is not a matter, as some would have it, of humanity just sitting around waiting for the Rapture. All time is the arena for the living out of the victory secured by Christ. The Church militant (as it used to be called with less embarrassment) is on the move to becoming the Church triumphant. Militancy is out of fashion today, and talk about triumph smacks of that Very Bad Thing called triumphalism. Yet Christians cannot, and should not try to, expunge the irrepressible sense of history as the drama of testing, battle, and contention for the truth that is nothing less than the story of the world. Lutheran theologian Robert Jenson has written impressively about how the world has lost its story, and how it is the mission of the Church to tell the story again, and to do so more convincingly by living the story that she tells.

Robert Louis Wilken writes in his essay on Gregory VII, "There is no past that does not have our present as its future, just as there is no future that will not have our present as its past." The second one thousand years that is the subject of this book is not only the story of Christians, nor only of Jews and Christians. But when in the following pages the authors say "our," they mean mainly the story of Christians and Jews. And because Christians were, however variously, in charge during the second one thousand years, it is the story of Jews mainly in relation to Christians. Today's sensitivity to "multiculturalism" is in many ways admirable, but it should not lead us to falsify history. The last one thousand years are, in largest part, the story of what William McNeill in his fine history by that title called "the rise of the West." While intellectuals in the West may often forget or deny it, Muslims and others are keenly aware that the rise of the West is synonymous with the world-historical dominance of the Christian West.

The conventional wisdom is that that story has come to an end. Christendom is a thing of the past. In my judgment, that is by no means self-evident. Certainly it is not self-evident to Islamic thinkers who see today's "globalization" on a historical continuum with the Crusades that began at the start of the second millennium. Such thinkers oscillate between declaring the Christian West to be morally decadent and exhausted, on the one hand, or to be an unstoppable juggernaut of Christian conquest, on the other. No doubt both claims are exaggerated, but that does not mean they should not be taken seriously. In this connection, I think we are well guided by the admittedly controversial but persuasive thesis of Harvard's Samuel Huntington regarding a "clash of civilizations" as the conceptual framework for thinking about the century and centuries ahead.

In any event, such are the considerations that guided the editors of *First Things* in putting together these essays on the second one thousand years. It is not true that those who forget history are doomed to repeat it, for history, by its very nature, cannot be repeated. But it is the fact that those who forget history cannot coherently think about what we ought to do or be in the future because they have forgotten who the "we" is. The editors chose to treat the second millennium century by century, choosing one figure as the prism, so to speak, through which to view each century. There is no suggestion that these are "representative" figures. At least in some instances, they are figures who posited themselves against what might be taken as representative of their time. But in such cases, what was characteristic of a historical period can be best illumined by those who recognized and opposed the "spirit of the times."

To speak of a "second one thousand years" is at least to hint at the possibility that there will be a third thousand years, and maybe a fourth, and only God knows how many after that. Only God needs to know. The personalities and the times limned in the following chapters help us to understand where we have come so far. Each chapter, and the book as a whole, assumes that these people and these times are part of a continuing "we." There is, in other words, an assumption of communal solidarity, even of friendship, with these people and these times. "Remember when?" each chapter asks. Friendship is in very large part remembering when. The story that is ours is — despite tumultuous disagreement and sometimes bloody conflict — a story of friendship in this crucial respect: We know that the humanity of which we are part has been ultimately befriended by the God of Abraham, Isaac, Jacob, and Jesus. All of the authors and most of the subjects of this book share that foundational belief. If it is a true belief, there are few things more important to the beginning of the third one thousand years than remembering the second one thousand years.

Gregory VII and the Politics of the Spirit

ROBERT LOUIS WILKEN

E VERY MARKING OF TIME has an arbitrariness about it, yet there seems to be something so large in its proportions about the commencement of a year that begins a century that inaugurates a millennium that it beguiles otherwise reasonable folk to imagine they are prophets. It is a temptation to be resisted. As enticing as it is to don the mantle of the seer and predict what will happen in the century to come, the greater part of wisdom is to look back, even far back, and greet the future with eyes focused by the past. The gift of discernment must be learned and if our eyes have not been trained to make out where we have been, they will be insentient to what is yet to be.

As we look back, however, what we see will be filtered inevitably through the prism of our own time. For there is no past that does not have our present as its future, just as there is no future that will not have our present as its past. The story is told of the distinguished French medievalist, Jean Leclercq, who was interviewed by journalists at Boston's Logan airport on his arrival in the United States for a lecture tour. One member of the press raised his hand and asked: "Tell me, sir, what century do you think was the most important?" Leclercq listened intently to the question, paused for a moment, and then softly replied: "Dees wun!"

No apology is needed to begin with the present. So let us first fasten on those things in former times that seem uncannily familiar to sensibilities attuned to the experiences of our century. The exercise should prove an instructive introduction to the topic at hand, the great pope of the eleventh century, Gregory VII.

In thinking about the eleventh century, the first century of the present millennium, consider the following:

The Crusades began in the eleventh century. In 1095 Pope Urban II preached his famous sermon to a large crowd in a meadow in Clermont, France, calling on Christians of the West to come to the aid of their brothers and sisters in the East and to recover the holy city of Jerusalem for Christian civilization. Four centuries earlier, in 634, Muslim armies had burst without warning out of the deserts of Arabia to conquer Damascus (635), Jerusalem (638), and other Christian cities in the Middle East, and within a few short years the vanguard of the new religion had swiftly swept across the ancient Christian lands, Palestine, Syria, Asia Minor (Turkey), Egypt, North Africa (Tunisia, Algeria), only to be stopped by Charles Martel in 732 at the battle of Poitiers in southern France.

In the face of such energy and determination the settled Christian world, with the exception of Constantinople, seemed defenseless, and a great curtain was soon drawn across the Mediterranean Sea, Christianity on the northern shore, Islam on the eastern and southern shores. Not until the eleventh century was Christian civilization capable of mounting a countermovement. Many in the West today, embarrassed by the militancy and brutality of the Crusades, would prefer to forget them, but the idea of liberating the Holy Land united Europe in a collective effort that altered the course of our history. And Islam has not forgotten the Crusades. When Mehmet Ali Agca tried to kill the Pope in May 1981 a letter was found among his papers with the words: "I have decided to kill John Paul II, supreme commander of the Crusades."

Item: The conflict between Christianity and Islam promises to be the dominant religious struggle at the start of the new millennium.

The eleventh century also gave birth to scholasticism, a way of reasoning that was to shape the course of Western philosophy and theology through the seventeenth century and even into modern times. St. Anselm, the most original Christian thinker between Augustine in the fifth century and Thomas Aquinas in the thirteenth century, was born in 1033 and his intellectual activity spanned the eleventh century. His philosophical essays *Monologion* and *Proslogion* and his theological treatise *Cur Deus Homo* (Why God Became Man) helped lay the foundation for the great flowering of Western thought in the next three centuries.

Item: At the end of the twentieth century and the beginning of the new millennium we are witnessing a major rethinking of the nature of human reason, and in particular how it functions in religious thought. The hegemony of the Enlightenment model of autonomous and critical reason, reason disengaged from its object, is swiftly coming to an end. We are, perhaps, living at a time when the understanding of reason and its relation to faith will be transformed as profoundly as it was in Anselm's day. Recently Pope John Paul II issued a new encyclical, *Fides et Ratio*. It may be the last papal encyclical of the millennium, and it is not insignificant that it deals with the relation of faith and reason, anticipating a discussion that will certainly accelerate in the new century.

The eleventh century was a period of intense spiritual vitality, particularly within the monastic communities. Monasticism changes the society even as it retreats from the world, and the changes in the monasteries provided the immediate background for the reforms of the popes. At the Benedictine monastery at Cluny in France, under the leadership of abbots Odilo and Hugh, a great reform movement reached the zenith of its influence in the Church and on society. St. Bernard, one of the most charismatic figures in Christian history, was born in 1090, and the Cistercians, the monastic movement with which he became associated, was founded in 1098 at Citeaux (*Cistercium* in Latin, hence the name Cistercians) by Robert of Molesme. Within a few decades the Cistercians, who practiced a more austere (and in their view more authentic) form of Benedictine monasticism, established hundreds of religious communities all over Europe where men and women quietly pursued a life of prayer and contemplation. Over the centuries contemplative monasticism as represented by the Benedictines and Cistercians has displayed remarkable staying power and today remains a vital feature of Christian life.

Item: At the turn of the millennium even activist Americans are discovering the contemplative side of religion, as books about its many offshoots — meditation, centering prayer, solitude, and silence — beckon the browser in the religion and spirituality sections of our bookstores. In her best-selling book *Dakota: A Spiritual Biography*, Kathleen Norris found a kinship between life in her parental home in an isolated town on the border of North and South Dakota and a Benedictine monastery. In places "where nothing ever happens, that the world calls dull," she learned, like the monks, to wait for God and listen. The success of her book suggests that it is a message many are eager to hear on the eve of the new century.

The eleventh century marked the official division between the Eastern Christian Churches, what is today known as Eastern Orthodoxy, and the

Catholic Church of the West claimed by Roman Catholicism and critiqued by the churches of the Reformation. For centuries these two large branches of Christianity had developed in different directions, in worship, in church organization, in language and culture, and in 1054 Rome and Constantinople formally broke off fellowship.

Item: As we look to the new millennium these two Christian communions are slowly and gingerly moving toward one another and looking anew at the obstacles that created and sustained the division, the *filioque* for example. It is too early to say that this deepest of all Christian divisions is beginning to heal, but there are signs that even if the twenty-first century does not bring reunion, it will lead to much closer rapprochement.

The eleventh century was a period of profound change and creativity in the understanding of ecclesiastical as well as civil law. For the first time in centuries legal scholars began to collect ancient Roman law codes, and at Bologna in northern Italy in the 1080s the inventive Guarnerius (Irnerius) attracted students from all over the Christian world to hear his lectures on Roman law. Prior to the eleventh century there was no concept of law as a body of principles, no one had attempted to organize and codify the prevailing laws, and there was no class of trained lawyers. Law had been seen as a product of the common conscience, not an expression of conscious reason or will, and legal scholars set about the task of reconciling contradictions, deriving principles, and drawing out conceptual implications of the ancient law codes. In the eleventh century law became a separate field of study with its own cadre of interpreters who applied the law to new areas of life.

Item: In our litigious society there is no area where the influence of the changes begun in the eleventh century is more obvious than in the practice of the law. Everything from the relation of members of a family to one another to the culture of the workplace in large corporations, from the great moral issues of our time to rights of professional athletes, becomes a matter to be adjudicated by lawyers and judges.

Yet, as significant as these developments were and continue to be, the commanding narrative of the eleventh century takes place in the life of a single person, a man who was more original than Anselm, more imperious than Bernard, and more courageous than a Crusader knight: the pope Gregory VII, also known as Hildebrand. So far-reaching was his effect on society and so eventful his influence on the Church that many have called him a revolutionary.

4

One historian considers his "revolution" the first of six that were to alter the course of Western society. In reverse chronological order they are the following: the Russian Revolution, the French Revolution, the American Revolution, the English revolution of the seventeenth century, the Protestant Reformation, and the papal revolution that began with Gregory's pontificate in 1073 and ended with the Concordat of Worms in 1122.

Just how deeply Gregory marked his age and the centuries to follow can be seen by sampling what some historians in recent generations have said about him. The social and economic historian Marc Bloch wrote: The Gregorian reform displayed "a spirit more revolutionary than contemporaries realized. . . . Its essence may be summed up in a few words: In a world where hitherto the sacred and profane had been almost inextricably mingled, the Gregorian reform proclaimed both the unique character and the supreme importance of the spiritual mission with which the Church was entrusted." Joseph Strayer identified Gregory's reforms with the origin and development of the idea of the modern secular state. Heinrich Mitteis spoke of a "constitutional revolution" and a "revolution in political thought." Yves Congar, the theologian, argued that "the reform begun by St. Leo IX (1049-1054) and continued with such vigor by St. Gregory VII represents a decisive turning point from the point of view of ecclesiastical doctrine in general and of the notion of authority in particular." Gerd Tellenbach had this to say: Pope Gregory VII "stands at the greatest . . . turning point in the history of Catholic Christendom. . . . He was at heart a revolutionary; reform in the ordinary sense of the world . . . could not satisfy him." And Harold Berman, who proposed the scheme of six revolutions, wrote: "The first of the great revolutions of Western history was the revolution against domination of the clergy by emperors, kings, and lords and for the establishment of the Church of Rome as an independent, corporate, political, and legal entity, under the papacy."

Gregory was born in a small town in Tuscany in Italy sometime between A.D. 1020-1025. As a boy he was sent to Rome to live in the Benedictine monastery of St. Mary on the Aventine hill. He took religious vows in the 1040s and in 1046 was asked to serve as chaplain to Pope Gregory VI, who had been sent into exile in Germany by King Henry III. Ironically, Gregory's life would also end in exile. On the death of Gregory VI in 1049 Hildebrand returned to Rome and was soon made administrator of the papal patrimony, the vast estates in central Italy governed directly by the pope. (In the eleventh century the popes were no less temporal rulers than the kings and princes who governed the kingdoms of Europe.) Under the two popes who immediately preceded him, Gregory served as archdeacon of the Church of Rome and was a guiding spirit in the reform efforts of the papacy. In 1073 he was elected pope.

The capital fact of ecclesiastical life in the early Middle Ages was that the affairs of the Church were managed by kings and princes. This interference in the Church's governance was not, however, viewed as a matter of political power muscling in on the authority of the Church; it was rather the king's duty. Like the kings of ancient Israel, medieval kings were anointed at their coronation and invested with a spiritual as well as political mission. Among the peoples of northern Europe — the Germans, Franks, Celts, Welsh, Irish, Danes, Bulgars, et al. — the only real authority was that of the king or prince or khan, and missionaries soon learned that the way to reach the people was through the mind and heart of the king, or sometimes the body of the queen. (Some Christian queens, it was reported, refused to sleep with their husbands until they converted.) These new Christian kings became the Church's defenders and bankers and overseers as they donated their own resources to build churches, endow monasteries, and in other ways lay the foundations for a Christian society. As the supreme religious head of the people, the king appointed bishops and abbots, ruled on religious and liturgical matters, and sometimes presided over ecclesiastical synods. Kings viewed the bishops as their *adjutores,* helpers. Christopher Dawson, the medieval historian, once remarked that Charlemagne viewed the pope as his private chaplain. It was the king's business to govern, said Charlemagne, that of the pope to pray.

The system of ecclesiastical organization developed in northern Europe fragmented the Church into regional jurisdictions defined by the territorial authority of the king or prince. Churches were often established by a wealthy landowner on land that was family property. Because the landowner constructed a church on his land out of his own funds, he considered the church his own property and reserved the right to nominate a priest to serve the people living on his land. Monasteries were expected to provide goods and revenue to the lord, and on occasion were used as dowries in royal marriages or as a source of soldiers for the prince's army.

The authority of the lord in ecclesiastical matters was symbolized by the practice of lay "investiture." This term originally referred to the ceremony in which a lord handed over land to a vassal in exchange for an oath of fealty. As a symbol of the transfer the lord would give the new vassal a staff or a sword or a spear. In time a similar practice developed at the installation of a bishop. At the time of consecration the king or his representative handed over the symbols of the office to the bishop (or abbot), usually a staff or crozier and a ring, and the king said: "Receive the church." The bishop was then consecrated in an ecclesiastical rite by other bishops, but the symbols of authority had been transmitted by the king, not the bishops. It was obvious that this system encouraged greater loyalty to the local lord than to the pope or to the Church as a universal communion.

Immediately before Gregory's pontificate, and with his strong support, his predecessors had mounted an active program of reform, focusing particularly on simony (the buying and selling of ecclesiastical offices) and on putting an end to clerical marriage (which encouraged seeking office for the financial rewards it offered the bishop's family). In 1049 celibacy was reaffirmed as mandatory for all clergy, and ten years later Pope Nicholas II laid down new rules that made the election of the pope the responsibility of the senior clergy of Rome, the cardinals (the term refers to the "hinges" between the bishop of Rome and the parishes), a practice that continues to this day (though cardinals today reside all over the world and merely hold title to parishes in Rome). By placing election of the pope solely in the hands of the cardinals, the new rules effectively excluded the emperor or a powerful king from controlling the election of a pope.

Even though Gregory had worked closely with his predecessors, he was dissatisfied with what they had accomplished. He was not a man of great learning, but he grasped what was before him in new ways. In his certitude about his mission, his decisiveness, and his personal charism, he stood apart from his fellows. His impatience with the pace of reform is evident in a letter he wrote to Hugo, abbot of the monastery at Cluny, two years after his election: "When I review in my mind the regions of the West, whether north or south, I find scarce any bishops who live or who were ordained according to law and who govern Christian people in the love of Christ and not for worldly ambition. And among secular princes I find none who prefer the honor of God to their own or righteousness to gain." A contemporary described Gregory as a tiger tensed for the leap.

The defining moment in Gregory's pontificate came over the election of a bishop in Milan in northern Italy, a city in the territory ruled by the German king Henry IV. At a synod in Rome in 1075, two years after his election as pope, Gregory issued a strongly worded condemnation of lay investiture. At first Henry IV, who hoped to be crowned emperor by the pope, was accommodating. But when a dispute erupted in Milan over the appointment of the bishop, the king intervened to insure the consecration of his own nominee. Neither the king nor the pope owned a character likely to allay strife. In a pointed letter Gregory reminded the king that he had no authority for such an action, and warned him that if he did not comply with the decree on lay investiture he would not only be excommunicated but also deposed. Here was a challenge without precedent. Popes had long been in the business of making kings and emperors, but no one imagined a pope could unmake a king. In Gregory's view a king forfeited his throne if he opposed apostolic decrees issued from Rome.

The king responded by calling his own council of German bishops who defiantly refused to bow to what they considered Gregory's imperious demands. One bishop was reported to have said that the pope ordered bishops around as though they were his bailiffs. The king labeled Gregory a "false monk" who had "incited subjects to rebel against their prelates" and behaved as though the kingdom was his to give and take away and not at the disposal of God. He urged the pope to step down. "Contrary to God's ordinance he desires to be king and priest at once." In words as mordant as anything Gregory wrote, the king taunted the pope with *"Descende, descende!"* ("Step down, step down!")

Undaunted, Gregory declared Henry excommunicate and deposed him as king. In a letter defending his actions, he dwelt solely on the excommunication, tacitly acknowledging that he might have overstepped his authority in deposing the king. But the spiritual ban alarmed the bishops and nobles who had supported Henry. Within months they began to withdraw their fealty to Henry and urged him to seek absolution from the pope. They issued an invitation for the pope to come to a council at Augsburg in Germany.

But when the pope reached northern Italy the promised escort had not arrived, and he took refuge in the castle of his friend Countess Matilda at Canossa. Here the famous confrontation between pope and king took place. The king, abandoned by his nobles and bishops, decided to approach the pope as a penitent and ask forgiveness. In January 1077, in the dead of winter, he crossed the Alps and after reaching the courtyard of the castle where the pope was staying, the king stood barefoot in the snow for three days waiting for Gregory to respond.

So unforgettable was the confrontation at Canossa that it has entered indelibly into the memory of Western civilization, especially among its statesmen and religious leaders. Some invoked Canossa when Fidel Castro met the Pope in Havana. In the Kulturkampf between Prussia and the Church in nineteenth-century Germany, Bismarck is reported to have said, "We will not go to Canossa." There, at a castle in the mountains of northern Italy, the two great authorities of medieval society, pope and emperor, priest and king, *sacerdotium* and *imperium,* met face-to-face, each testing the other. The conventional retelling of the story focuses on the king standing barefoot in the courtyard, but the real drama may have been taking place in the pope's chambers within the castle. The three days' wait was as much a sign of Gregory's irresolution as of the king's humility. Gregory knew full well that the king had made the journey in part because of his dwindling support in Germany, but once the political winds shifted, as they certainly would if he were absolved, the king could hardly be expected to be so compliant. Yet Henry came as a son of the Church asking absolution. How could a priest turn away a penitent? Finally the pope called for him, the castle doors were opened, and the king was granted absolution — not, however, without the pope extracting an oath from the king that he would abide by papal decisions in the future.

By coming to Canossa and submitting to Gregory, Henry acknowledged the pope's right to judge kings. But Gregory's victory was chimerical — at least in the short run. Once Henry was granted absolution, he returned to Germany as king, legitimated by the pope. In the meantime, however, Henry's enemies had elected a new king and presented the pope with a dilemma. Whom should he recognize? Unfortunately, Gregory chose the new king, Rudolph; he even imprudently predicted Henry's imminent death. Henry, however, remained robustly healthy, while Rudolph died in battle. This was a costly misstep and an ominous portent. Never again would Gregory regain his balance. Soon opinion began to shift away from the pope toward Henry, and the king, riding a wave of popularity, appointed an anti-pope (Clement III). Abandoned by his cardinals, Gregory was forced to take refuge in the Castel Sant'Angelo in Rome near the Vatican, under the protection of the hated Normans who had occupied and sacked the city. He finally fled to Norman territory in the south of Italy, a state he would not have recognized a few years earlier. In May 1085 Gregory died in Salerno with the words of the psalmist on his lips, "'I have loved justice and hated iniquity'; for that reason I die in exile." Ironically, the pope who most identified with St. Peter did not die *apud sanctum Petrum.*

Clearly the measure of Gregory's greatness is not to be sought in the immediate events that ended his pontificate. When he died there were few signs that his policies would triumph. Yet he knew the future belonged to him, and in his letters he seemed conscious his words would one day become authoritative. To some his final words are taken as a cry of defeat, even despair, but they might just as well be read as a shout of victory. Martyrdom is not a sign of defeat. "Blessed are those who are persecuted for the sake of justice, for theirs is the kingdom of heaven," said Jesus in the Beatitudes. Gregory's words have been taken as an apt epitaph for martyrs, and they appear often in collections of famous last words. The great Belgian historian Henri Pirenne, who was deported to Germany during World War I, said that he found comfort in Gregory's final words during his exile in Germany. As Gregory had demanded that kings and princes be obedient to truth, so he willingly imposed the same conditions on himself, remaining faithful to the end.

But, one might ask, faithful to what? Gregory would have said: to the freedom of the Church, an *ecclesia libera, casta, et catholica*, a Church that is free, pure, and catholic. His predecessors had centered their reform efforts on simony and clerical marriage, and Gregory was not indifferent to these problems. But the circumstances of his pontificate as well as his own genius led him to frame the issues in a new way. In his hands reform was not primarily an affair of the moral or spiritual life; it had to do with the right ordering of Church and society. In a radical departure from recent ecclesiastical custom, Gregory had stripped the king of his spiritual authority and reduced him to the status of a simple layman. The old complementarity of pope and emperor came to an end. Once the king had been directly accountable to God; now he was accountable to the pope.

By desacralizing the authority of the king, Gregory disengaged the spiritual world from political control (at least in theory) and set in motion forces that would alter not only the self-understanding of the Church but also of the state. The medieval kingdoms were religious states and the king, as head of the people, was the supreme authority in religious as well as in political matters. If spiritual governance was now solely in the hands of the bishops and pope, kingship had to be understood differently and new foundations laid for the political authority of the state. Paradoxically, as the Church became a sovereign body with its own head, administrative structure, body of law, and courts, its very existence gave impetus to new political ideas that would eventually give rise to the modern state. As the medieval historian K. Leyser has written, "Political ideas in the classical sense only appear in the polemics of the eleventh and early twelfth centuries incoherently, in flashes. . . . There [was at that time] no theory of the secular state as such, but as a result of the great crisis it was all ready to be born." Deprived of its spiritual authority, the state was forced to conceive of itself anew as a corporate body independent of the Church. In this sense the origins of the modern (and secular) state are to be traced to Gregory VII and the Investiture Controversy.

Gregory knew that the customs prevailing in the Church and society in his day had no foundation in ancient Christian tradition. In one of his letters he says: "Christ did not say 'I am custom,' but 'I am truth.'" The words are not original. They go back to Augustine, and can be found in earlier writers, Cyprian and Tertullian. But their application is new. What was considered ancient tradition, Gregory denominated custom — practices that had developed over the last several centuries in northern Europe. They were not apostolic. Like all great figures in the Church's history, Gregory knew that faithfulness did not mean slavish obedience to current practice. Faithfulness to tradition, by contrast to preservation of custom, required discernment of the deeper meaning of the faith amidst the vicissitudes of time. By challenging the customs of his time Gregory wished to build a bridge over the centuries to the more authentic truths that animate Christian life.

Gregory's letters reproach the king with pronouncements on the freedom of the Church. "Let him [Henry] no longer imagine that Holy Church is his subject or his handmaid but rather let him recognize her as his superior and his mistress." He speaks plainly and bluntly, eschewing euphemisms. But his imperiousness is not just a polemical strategy. He has a vision of the Church as a corporate and sovereign body in its own right. Christianity is not just the spiritual dimension of the social order; it creates its own social and political order. Bishops and pope, not princes, constitute the Church; they, not kings, stand in succession from the apostles. Only bishops can invest bishops in their office; kings have no such authority. Investiture, if you will, comes from Christ; it is not mediated by the king. The authority of the bishop is not conferred from above; it comes through the line of bishops stretching back through time to the apostles and to Christ. Hence the one who bears office is not simply a spokesman for the apostles; in his person he is their embodiment and sacramentally makes present the reality of Christ in the world.

Like any corporate body, the Church could not exist without a head. In 1075, two years after he became pope, Gregory jotted down a series of theses, a set of talking points for his own reference to be drawn on in letters or set forth in canonical form in papal decrees. Some of the points are the following: That the Roman bishop alone is by right called universal; that his legate, even if of lower grade, takes precedence in a council over all bishops and may render a sentence of deposition against them; that the Bishop of Rome alone may depose and reinstate bishops; that to him alone is it permitted to make new laws according to the needs of the times; that he may depose emperors; that no judgment of his may be revised by anyone, and that he alone may revise the judgments of all.

On first reading Gregory's theses sound revolutionary, and there can be no question that in the annals of the Church's earlier history there is nothing to match these extraordinary claims. Yet it was only as Gregory was faced with specific cases that he invoked his principles, and he was careful to document his claims by citing earlier canonical authorities and precedents. He saw, as no one had before him, that the pope had to be more than a symbolic head of the Church. The Bishop of Rome was not simply the court of last appeal; the pope was called to *govern* the universal Church. He alone was charged to care for all the churches. Unless the Church of Rome actually bound the churches in every part of the world together in an organic body and the pope exercised jurisdiction, all talk of the Church as a worldwide communion — i.e., as catholic — was illusory. The Church needs a real, not honorary, head.

Gregory had a kind of mystic identification with St. Peter. When his decrees are disregarded he says that Peter has been offended; he presides over synods "under the power of St. Peter"; he forbids a candidate for bishop to accept the office "by the apostolic authority of St. Peter"; and he asks bishops to "swear fealty to St. Peter." So complete is the identification with St. Peter that he speaks of Peter "now living in the flesh." In defending his deposition of Henry he cites the words of Jesus: "You are Peter and on this rock I will build my Church, and the gates of Hell shall not prevail against it. I will give you the keys of the kingdom of Heaven and whatever you bind on earth shall be bound in Heaven and whatever you loose on earth shall be loosed in Heaven" (Matthew 16:18). And then he asks, "Are kings excepted here? Do they not belong to the sheep which the Son of God committed to St. Peter?"

Because Christ had given the rule of the Church to one man, Gregory reasoned that the Church was not a communion of local churches; it was a universal fellowship apostolic in origin and catholic in scope. Peter not only symbolized the unity of the Church, his authority allowed the pope to govern as its head. "God gave the power of binding and loosing in heaven and on earth to St. Peter" — and, Gregory adds, *principaliter,* as prince. As these ideas began to take root in the consciousness of the bishops and popes who followed him, the Church acted more and more as an independent corporation defined legally and administratively.

There was, however, a price to be paid. By conceiving of the Church in constitutional and juridical terms, albeit for the purposes of liberating the clergy to carry out their spiritual activities, Gregory set in motion ideas that subtly altered the way the Church was understood. In the centuries that followed, as canon lawyers scoured earlier sources to provide a legal basis for papal authority, the Church came to be viewed less as a spiritual fellowship than as a hierarchical and juridical corporation composed of clergy and bishops and pope. Gregory has little to say about the laity in his letters, and his reforms helped create a sense of the clergy as a distinct class united with the pope but separated from the laity, who occupy a lower place.

Yet Gregory's preoccupation with the constitution of the Church cannot be dismissed simply as an unwelcome inheritance from medieval times that needs, in a more enlightened age, to be displaced by a spiritual conception of the Church. Religion, like culture, does not float free of institutions. Without the discipline of law and the structure of institutional life, our energies are dissipated and our lives impoverished. Whatever else the Church is, it is very much an institution. Nor are institutions simply instrumental. They tutor our affections and lift us beyond ourselves. As Cardinal Newman once remarked, we need objects on which our "holier and more generous feelings may rest. . . . Human nature is not republican." It is one of the persistent falsehoods of our time that the less institutional the Church, the more spiritual it will be.

Augustine's metaphor for the Church was a "city," and one way of reading his great work the *City of God* is to see it as a defense of the social and even political character of Christianity. Christianity is not a set of ideas, it is a new kind of community. The philosophers, wrote Augustine, had taught that the "happy life is social." But "we insist on that even more strongly than they." "How could that City have made its first start, how could it have advanced along its course, how could it attain its appointed

13

goal, if the life of the saints were not social?" What Augustine expressed theologically about the Church, Gregory VII understood juridically and legally. His genius was to discern that this body, this society, this city, required constitutional form. That his legacy, under different circumstances, may have seemed at times to alter in questionable ways the character of the community whose life he sought to order does not diminish the profundity of his insight nor obscure the clarity of his vision.

The Mind of Maimonides

DAVID NOVAK

ABOUT MOSES MAIMONIDES there is an old Jewish folk saying: "From Moses to Moses there was none like Moses." No one brought forth the teaching of Moses and his prophetic and rabbinic successors more comprehensively and systematically than did Maimonides. More has been said and written about him than any other Jewish thinker throughout history. Indeed, many great debates since his death have revolved around the question of just who interpreted Maimonides correctly and who did not. To get Maimonides right has been for many to get Judaism right. His role in the history of Jewish thought is comparable to the role of Thomas Aquinas in Catholic thought. Just as Aquinas (who was influenced by Maimonides) treated with respect all great theologians and philosophers irrespective of religious differences with them, Maimonides did the same with the pagans, Christians, and Muslims, saying about them: "Accept the truth, whatever its source." Indeed, Maimonides himself is a marvelous companion for anyone searching for truth. He could well be considered the outstanding thinker of the twelfth century in the West. His unsurpassed contributions to both Judaism and Western thought left neither quite the same.

His actual name was Moses son of Rabbi Maimon the Spaniard, "Maimonides" being the name his Latin translators gave him, namely, "son of Maimon." (Jews have traditionally referred to him by the acronym *Rambam*.) We know very little about his early life. He was born in 1135 into a distinguished family of rabbinic scholars in Cordoba in Andalus, then part of Muslim (or "Moorish") Spain. His father was his first and most significant teacher. No doubt he was a very precocious youth; he wrote a treatise on proper linguistic usage of theological terms that he probably completed around the age of sixteen. Because of the persecution of non-Muslims by the fanatical Almohad sect, Maimonides and his family were forced to leave Spain when he was in his late teens. They wandered for years in North Africa, where it seems they frequently had to pose as Muslims. After living for a time in the land of Israel, the family finally settled permanently in Fustat, the old city of Cairo in Egypt.

It was Maimonides' good fortune that he did not have to earn a living during his intellectually formative years; his older brother David, a wealthy pearl merchant, supported him. But David died in a shipwreck in the Indian Ocean when Moses was about thirty and his comfortable life was shattered, both financially and emotionally. For about a year, it seems, he remained sunk in a deep depression, during which time he accomplished almost nothing. Eventually his emotional health was restored, and his highly creative career thenceforth moved on at a steady pace. (His advice concerning the treatment of melancholia bears the unmistakable stamp of personal experience and practice.)

Until rather late in the Middle Ages, rabbis were not paid for their services — since Moses taught the Torah for free, so should his successors. For that reason, Maimonides like any other rabbi had to adopt a profession in the world, and like many intellectually gifted medieval rabbis he became a physician. His medical reputation seems to have grown with his reputation as a teacher of the Jewish tradition. His speciality was gastroenterology and a number of short treatises he wrote have survived and are useful even today, due to his emphasis on preventive medicine. His advice on proper diet and healthy activities has a very contemporary ring to it. He rose to become the court physician to the political head of his society, the Sultan, and to his court. He was also the acknowledged religious leader of his own Egyptian Jewish community. Soon his fame spread to other Jewish communities, whose leaders consulted him about the most significant questions of law and theology — although a number of Jewish authorities bitterly opposed him as a dangerous radical. For years he maintained a grueling professional schedule, combining his medical practice, community leadership, scholarship, teaching, and an international correspondence.

The last few years of his life were devoted to what we would call today a charity clinic. It seems that he regarded his main intellectual work to have by then been completed and he wanted to devote the rest of his life to putting into practice the theory of *imitatio Dei* he had presented at the end of his major work in philosophical theology, the *Guide of the Perplexed.* Maimonides died in 1204, and, according to tradition, was buried in Tiberius in the land of Israel. His immediate intellectual successor was his only son, Abraham, a gifted scholar though no match for his father.

Aside from treatises and responsa on a variety of religious and scientific topics, Maimonides wrote three major works. His first was a commentary on the *Mishnah,* which is the second-century compendium upon which the discussions in the Talmud are based. Next to Scripture, the *Mishnah* is the most important book in Judaism. Though it is called a "commentary," this first great work of Maimonides is actually more of a digest of the main points of the *Mishnah* and their subsequent development in the Talmud than it is an actual line-by-line exegesis of an older text. It could well be seen as preparatory for his second major work, what Maimonides himself called "our great compilation," *Mishneh Torah,* the fourteen-volume systematization of all Jewish law from Scripture to his own day. (The relation of the first work to the second work could be compared to Aquinas's commentary on the *Sentences* of Peter Lombard in relation to his "great compilation," the *Summa Theologiae.*) *Mishneh Torah* is a theological as well as a legal work; Maimonides thought that Jewish theology, itself mandated by the law, should aspire to the precision that characterizes discussions of the law.

Finally, there is his third great work, *Guide of the Perplexed,* the product of his later period. It is devoted to what he considered to be the most important philosophical questions concerning Jewish theology, especially as those questions relate to the text of Scripture. *The Guide,* when translated from its original Arabic into Hebrew during Maimonides' lifetime, became the most important work in philosophical theology for Jews thereafter; and when it was translated into Latin shortly after his death, it was taken most seriously by Aquinas and a number of later Christian thinkers. (The irony of this fame is that Maimonides wrote the *Guide* for only a select number of his disciples, those worthy of being initiated into the "secrets of the Torah.") *The Guide* is also the book that the renegade from Judaism, Baruch Spinoza, felt had to be overcome if philosophy was ever to become independent of revelation.

Maimonides' work itself might be seen as a response to three challenges to his understanding of Judaism: (1) the Jewish tradition itself, (2) Greek natural science, metaphysics, and ethics/politics ("philosophy" in the broad Platonic-Aristotelian sense) as transmitted through Arabic sources, and (3) Christianity and Islam.

The Jewish tradition, itself built upon the discussions of the ancient rabbis in the Talmud and related literature, posed the greatest difficulty for the philosophical mind of Maimonides. The challenge was to organize in an architectonic structure a vast body of data that, on the surface anyway, appears to be hopelessly disjointed and even random. Others before him had tried to tackle this problem — most notably, Isaac Alfasi as regards the legal data and Saadiah Gaon as regards the theological data. Their impressive efforts were still piecemeal compared to that of Maimonides. Alfasi essentially paraphrased rabbinic texts (and not on every subject at that), and gave them a partial topical order. Maimonides was convinced that the philosophical assumptions of Saadiah were too eclectic to sustain the truly systematic theology the Torah required. For these philosophical assumptions Maimonides turned to Plato, the Arabic neo-Platonist Alfarabi, and even more to Aristotle and the Arabic neo-Aristotelian Ibn Sina (Avicenna).

Although not a slavish follower of Aristotle by any means, as we shall soon see, Maimonides was nevertheless convinced by Aristotle's assumption of universal teleology, i.e., that every living entity in the universe has a natural final state. Creatures below the moon begin moving toward their destiny at birth and continue a linear developmental trajectory consummated and sustained in maturity, what Aristotelians see as a movement from potency to act. In plants and animals, such movement is unconscious and instinctual, frustrated only by external impediments. In humans, however, that movement is conscious and to a certain extent free, and thus can be frustrated by bad choices as well.

Between God, who transcends all creaturely categories (hence Maimonides' famous assertion that we can only speak negatively about God, i.e., what he is not rather than what he is), and humans stand the heavenly bodies. These bodies are themselves higher intelligences, living beings who orbit in an unending circle motored by their unending and perfect knowledge of God. These intelligences, traditionally called "angels," are the models to which humans aspire in their quest for the *summum bonum* — to know God. Maimonides likens the righteous who attain this in the world-to-come to such angels in their beatific consummation. What the angels are, humans desire to become.

In this world, the immediate task of humans is to discover just what acts contribute to this overall process and how to perform them properly.

Jews discover this in the Torah, the tradition stemming from it, and what also is constructed for the sake of the ends of the Torah. Thus Maimonides' positive task as a theologian-jurist was to justify intellectually the commandments of the Torah and the supplementary edicts of the rabbis. He used teleology as the principle which both ordered and applied the law. Here Maimonides' thought is the most significant point of development in the rabbinic doctrine of the "reasons of the commandments." But whereas many of the rabbis assumed that only some of the commandments have reasons intelligible to human minds, Maimonides was convinced that all of the commandments have such reasons. To assume anything less would be to imply that God has less wisdom than a wise human lawgiver.

The difference between reason and revelation is not between what is intelligible and what is inherently "mysterious." Reason is an arduous step-by-step process that attempts to understand the content revealed in a prophetic event. For Maimonides, prophecy is something possible (but not voluntary, ultimately being a gift of grace) for any human being, that is, any human being first possessing some very high moral and intellectual prerequisites. Much of this sounds quite similar to how the philosopher-guardians of Plato's *Republic* first ascend an intellectual ladder by means of dialectic until some of them see with the eye of the intellect the supreme form: the Good. This similarity is no accident, inasmuch as Maimonides' political theory was heavily influenced by Arabic Platonism.

Disagreeing with one prominent rabbinic opinion, Maimonides did not regard the possibility of prophecy to have vanished with the destruction of the Second Temple in A.D. 70, and unlike a great theological predecessor a century earlier, Judah Halevi, he did not regard true prophecy to be confined to the Jews. The superiority of Jewish prophecy to him is a difference of degree rather than of kind. This was important, as we shall soon see, in Maimonides' treatment of Christianity and Islam, the two other monotheistic faiths.

Maimonides' teleology is constituted at two levels. At the first level, he attempts to discern what might be called the "perennial" reasons of the commandments, those based on permanent features of human nature pertaining either to the relationship with God or to relationships among human persons in society. The former he called the "repair of the soul"; the second he called the "repair of the body" (as in the body politic). As an example of his reasoning on this first level, he notes that even though there are worse crimes than murder — especially idolatry, which unlike murder or any other prohibition is exceptionless — human society must take the prohibition of murder most seriously since without it even a rudimentary human society is impossible. Indeed, Maimonides learned much about political order from both Plato and Aristotle, both of whom were at least participants in idolatry if not actually committed to it in spirit themselves. To cite another example, although the strict observance of the Sabbath is considered by the Talmud to be for Jews alone, Maimonides saw great human value in the way the Sabbath teaches human beings to appreciate divine creation of the universe and the way it creates true rest for human beings, enabling them to interact regularly with each other in a way based more on spiritual equality and less on physical inequality.

At the second level, Maimonides' teleology is much more historically contingent, for there are many details of the Torah that cannot be explained by their immediate value to human nature per se. About some of these details, such as those pertaining to intricacies of the sacrificial system or the system of ritual purity, Maimonides confesses ignorance. He admits that he can explain only more general institutions and not every particularity within them. Regarding institutions like the sacrificial system, whose reasons seem obscure, Maimonides resorts to a certain amount of historical speculation. He is convinced, for instance, that because of the Jewish people's long exposure to idolatrous practices with their emphasis on physical worship, the Torah could not have successfully commanded the Jews to adopt a purely spiritual form of worship, consisting solely in the adoration of the transcendent God. Essentially, the Torah had to make a kind of cultural compromise, keeping the form of worship to which the people were accustomed, but purging it of its idolatrous intentions. In this way, Maimonides seems to have followed the talmudic principle: the law has to take the evil inclination into consideration. Accordingly, the third main purpose of the Torah is to wean the people away from idolatry by not only prohibiting its theory and practice, but also ruling out the cultural symptoms of idolatry that have appeared in history, especially at the origins of Jewish history.

This does not mean, however, that Maimonides was thereby making the Torah into a historically contingent teaching. He regarded idolatry itself to be a perennial problem of human nature, because humans always need to relate themselves to their Creator, and there is a right way and a wrong way to do so. Maimonides thought that idolatry was often a more immediately attractive option to human beings than the proper worship of God, which is harder and more demanding of the intellect. Idolatry is an ineradicable human problem because it results from the inappropriate use of human imagination, and yet humans cannot very well live without imagination. That is why one can only treat the symptoms of idolatry at any given historical moment and hope that such treatment will prevent this endemic disease of human nature from worsening or spreading. For this reason one can see why there is no inconsistency between Maimonides' explanation of idolatry along the lines of cultural anthropology and his eschatological hope for the restoration of the Temple cult with its full system of animal sacrifice, a feature of the liturgy since long before Maimonides' time. The symptoms of idolatry are no accident and, hence, the ancient practices mandated by the Torah are still the best prophylactic against this treatable but permanently incurable disease.

In the Jewish tradition, idolatry, literally called *avodah zarah*, "strange worship," takes two forms. One form is the worship of "other" gods, a substitution for the one, unique, uncreated Infinity by something plural, generic, created, and finite. Such idolatry is the worship of those whom we call "pagans." For Maimonides, those who worship the heavenly intelligences are guilty of making absolute those forces which are under the total control of the one God. That is the essential difference between monotheism, of which Judaism is the highest but not the only example, and all polytheisms ancient and contemporary. The second form of idolatry, however, is a good deal more subtle than the pagan form, and is a constant temptation even to the adherents of monotheistic religions. For this form of idolatry does not err in the object of its worship but, rather, it errs in worshiping this true God in a way inconsistent with what little we know about God and his interest in the world.

For Maimonides, this second type of idolatry has its real origin in bad monotheistic theology that takes the anthropomorphic language of Scripture literally. Good theology takes scriptural language that attributes physical properties of God to be largely figurative. It is a concession to human imagination, which even philosophers have to deal with because of the humanity they share with all other humans. At most, what philosophical monotheists can do is reconstrue scriptural God-talk as being either an imaginatively appealing description of the effects of God's creative action on the world, or as a negation of ascribing to God any of the limitations of his creatures. For Maimonides, to say that "God is good" is to say either that God is the cause of what we take to be good in the world, or else to say that God is not bad.

At the practical level, Maimonides carried this out by attempting to purge Judaism of any superstitions he thought had accrued to it over the ages. He especially lacked patience for much of the poetry that had found its way into the liturgy. Like Plato, whose political philosophy had such an influence on his own political thought, it seems that Maimonides too would have banished the poets from the optimal city, which for him is the society constituted by the Torah. He could do only so much along these lines since some of this poetry was too ensconced in the tradition to be entirely rooted out.

Against this backdrop, the theology or theosophy of the *Kabbalah*, which began to appear after Maimonides' time, might well be seen as nothing less than the return of the repressed. Indeed, even today one can see the two main options in Jewish God-talk as being either Maimonidean or Kabbalistic. Whereas Kabbalah holds that all the language of revelation is a positive description of the inner life of God, Maimonides and his followers hold that the language of Scripture is about the world and only speaks of God by means of effect or negation (the *via negativa*).

Even though Maimonides did not think that all philosophers are necessarily prophets, he did think that all prophets are necessarily philosophers. "Philosophy" in Maimonides' day meant natural science, metaphysics, and ethics/politics. In terms of his theology, this meant that there could not be a lasting impasse between the truth derived from philosophy and the truth derived from the Torah. Thus philosophy in this full sense posed a great challenge to Maimonides. For it was philosophy that had perplexed Maimonides' student, Rabbi Joseph son of Rabbi Judah, and some others like him, and Maimonides intended in the *Guide,* which is addressed as an epistle to Rabbi Joseph, to lead them out of this spiritual dilemma.

The Torah might not be worldly in its origins and in its ultimate end; nevertheless, it is still in the world and must be understood by secular criteria. Like the world, the Torah is a created entity; as the rabbis put it, the Torah speaks in human language, a principle Maimonides reworked philosophically. The Torah, then, must be grasped in the same way one grasps created nature. Thus Maimonides would not have accepted, as many who have followed Kant have, that there is an absolute difference between the world constituted by natural science and the world constituted by those disciplines that include human action. Whereas Kant and his followers (and there have been many among Christians and Jews) could believe in a natural world in which everything is causally determined and a moral world in which there is freedom and call this impasse an antinomy, Maimonides and his followers could not accept freedom in the moral world unless there is also less than absolute determinism in the natural world.

In this area, Maimonides' main problem was what to do when the Torah and philosophy seem to contradict one another, which usually arose over issues of natural science. The most serious such contradiction Maimonides faced was that the Torah is traditionally interpreted to teach that the universe is the result of a pure act of divine creation, an act having no preconditions, hence creation "out of nothing." But Aristotle, who for Maimonides is the most convincing natural scientist, taught that the universe is eternal, without beginning and without end.

Here Maimonides boldly asserts that if Aristotle had convincingly demonstrated his theory of the eternity of the universe, then one would have to reinterpret the Torah accordingly (something that was actually done by the fourteenth-century Jewish theologian and natural scientist Gersonides). Maimonides had to say this since, for him, both the Torah and nature are created entities, hence subject to the same basic methodology to bring out their inherent intelligibility. And since we are in the world known by philosophy before we are able to receive the Torah (remember: the prophets must first be philosophers), the method for understanding the Torah is derived from our method for understanding the world, not vice versa. Maimonides accepted the authority of tradition only in matters of law. In matters of science, however — and he would consider most of theology to be a science — there are no authorities. One must be convinced by whatever is most rationally convincing here and now, however much it might go against traditionally accepted opinions. Accordingly, to the chagrin of a number of traditionalists, he refused to assign any authority at all to the natural science of the rabbis of the Talmud, even though he fully accepted their legal authority in providing indispensable rules and principles for current legal decision-making.

Nevertheless, despite this possibility of revising much of traditional creation theory along Aristotelian lines, Maimonides rejects the eternity of the world, not because he opts for tradition over Aristotle, but because Aristotle did not satisfactorily demonstrate his own thesis. Aristotle made an unconvincing (to Maimonides) inference from his natural science to a metaphysical conclusion. As a result, Aristotle's eternity thesis was just as plausible or implausible as the traditional Jewish (and Christian and Muslim thereafter) doctrine of creation ex nihilo. If so, then there is a historical advantage to sticking with the traditional view since when it comes to change, the burden of proof is more on those who would change than on those who would maintain the status quo.

Even though Maimonides could have left the question at that point, he wanted to move in an intellectually more satisfying direction. So he presses Aristotle on his own ground: teleology. Maimonides argues that Aristotle is not teleological enough. For whereas Aristotle could constitute an immanent teleology *in* the universe, he could not constitute a teleology *for* the universe. That is, he could not locate a purpose for the universe as a whole. He could not do that because his God is too immanent; his God is still part of the universe, even if at its very apex.

For Maimonides, only a God who utterly transcends the universe could have created it with a purpose that transcends anything internal to it: the purpose is to know God. This transcendence of cosmic purpose and the transcendence of God are correlated. The teleology that Aristotle partially, and so accurately, constituted *in* the world is now to be constituted as being given *to* the world as a whole from beyond. Thus Maimonides shows that not only is the doctrine of creation not at odds with cosmic teleology, it actually carries it beyond the limitations of Aristotle's theory. Maimonides never says that creation out of nothing can be proved. For how could it be proved when proof is what can be shown in a relation of entities within the world itself? Nevertheless, creation theory provides an overall paradigm that brings out more of the intelligibility of the universe precisely because it can relate it as a whole to what is beyond it. Hence a doctrine of faith helps expand the very horizon of reason.

Maimonides' approach to the two other monotheistic faiths, Christianity and Islam, is quite similar to his approach to philosophy. (He saw no value at all in polytheistic faiths.) Like philosophy, Christianity and Islam are true when they are variations of themes most completely presented in Judaism; and they are in error when they contradict Judaism. Furthermore, like his treatment of philosophy and, indeed, like his treatment of Judaism itself, Maimonides judges these other communities based on a criterion of the relation of theory and practice. On this central point, Maimonides is very much the Platonist and not the consistent Aristotelian some scholars have thought him to be.

In the *Republic*, Plato sees the philosopher-guardian's function to be both practical and theoretical. He is to provide the best possible practical rule of the polity because of his insight into the theoretical foundations of the good life, and he is to provide the practical means for would-be philosophers to be able to pursue the true life of the intellect. Theory (in Greek, "to gaze" — in Plato's usage to gaze at the eternal Forms) grounds practice, and practice is for the sake of theory. Practical excellence without theoretical excellence gives us competent politicians without real vision, and theoretical excellence without practical excellence gives us incompetent dreamers. For Aristotle, conversely, such a combination is an impossibility because practical excellence makes one see theory as unrealistic and theoretical excellence makes one see practice as boring. Nevertheless, for Maimonides, what might not be possible in a purely human polity, especially one with an erroneous theological tradition, is possible in a polity directly related to God through prophecy. Instead of accepting Aristotle's political skepticism, Maimonides carries Plato's politics even further, doing what he did to Aristotle's metaphysics, namely, carrying it beyond its original limits. Maimonides is quite clear that a normative teaching is considered divine not so much because of its origins in revelation, but, rather, because it directs a human community to ends first human ("the repair of the body"), then divine ("the repair of the soul"). By this criterion Judaism becomes the best divine law, but not the only one.

Within this overall scheme, one can see Maimonides' consistent treatment of Islam, a religious community he lived under all his life. Maimonides sees the relation of Islam to Judaism as primarily theoretical. With the strict monotheism of Islam, Maimonides has no quarrel. Indeed, he could not have formulated his monotheistic theology if he had not learned his philosophical method for theology from Muslims. Maimonides finds fault, however, with the practical politics of Muslim regimes. He considered Islamic ethics and politics to be inferior to their Jewish counterparts. As much as he possibly could as a second-class citizen in a Muslim society, Maimonides expressed his displeasure with the decided lack of virtue in the way Muslims rule their societies and relate to one another.

Concerning Christianity, with which he probably had no real contact, Maimonides' views underwent a decided change over time. In his aversion to what he considered to be Christian dilutions of pure monotheism, especially in its doctrine of the Trinity, much of Maimonides' philosophical critique of Christian theology is similar to Islamic arguments against it. In his earlier work, Maimonides translated his theoretical disdain of Christianity into practice. He deemed Christians to be idolators and bemoaned the fact that political necessity forced many European Jews to live in Christian societies.

Nevertheless, this is not the whole picture. At the end of his great code, *Mishneh Torah,* in his discussion of the political-legal role of the Messiah-to-come, Maimonides makes a predictable concession to Islam, but a surprising concession to Christianity. He argues that despite the errors of Jesus and Muhammad, the religions that emerged from their respective teachings are instruments of divine providence for bringing all of humankind to the worship of the one true God. Now it is obvious from this concession to Christianity that he no longer regarded it to be a form of idolatry, the worship of a "strange" god. Surely no form of radical idolatry could possibly be the means for the universal spread of monotheism. (Ironically enough, the Christian censors of the printed editions of *Mishneh Torah* forced the publishers to remove that passage.)

Moreover, in a responsum written after the publication of *Mishneh Torah,* Maimonides rules that Jews may teach the Torah to Christians but not to Muslims because Christians believe Hebrew Scripture *in toto* to be the revealed word of God, whereas Muslims believe that primary text to be the Quran; for them, Hebrew Scripture is a flawed revelation. Thus Jews and Christians share a common revelation in a way that Jews share with no other religious community. Furthermore, Maimonides believes that Jews can best proselytize Christians because of this common text. All Jews need do is show Christians how they have misinterpreted that common text (the New Testament being the erroneous Christian interpretation or *midrash* he has in mind) and how Judaism's interpretation of it is ultimately more convincingly accurate. (Using the same logic, Christians have frequently regarded Jews as the most logical objects of their own proselytizing efforts.) The Jewish problem with Christianity, for Maimonides, is largely a matter of exegesis, and the differences there are more theoretical than practical. True idolators, on the other hand, could hardly have accepted Hebrew Scripture as the word of God.

So, what is Maimonides' legacy? For Jews, Maimonides is such a part of the tradition that he has long been inextricable from it. But he also has a legacy for those who are not part of these intimately Jewish conversations. That legacy, it seems to me, is his methodology. He was convinced that the highest human task, from the first humans in the Garden of Eden to the righteous in the world-to-come, is to pursue truth. Here and now that pursuit is to be conducted in the created order, which includes the historical communities in which we live and from whose members we have learned to speak, most importantly about God. That created order consists of the findings of reason and what revelation teaches. The way we understand our world and the way we understand revelation is the same. Such a process of understanding need not accept any obscurity from the authorities of the past. The human intellect is free to soar as long as it understands that a goal awaits its efforts and that it is responsible to the other humans similarly engaged — wherever and whenever they happen to have been situated. To claim to be able to speak *de novo* about anything, much less about God, as Descartes and his followers have claimed, would have struck Maimonides as utterly unnatural.

It is a mistake of many current followers of Maimonides to think they can conduct the search for truth using the same tools he used. Maimonides relied on philosophical paradigms of his own day (especially cosmic teleology) that have long since lost their value for us at a different point in history. Indeed, Maimonides himself advised us to use the most coherent philosophical paradigms at hand, and for us that must include the findings of both the natural and the human sciences (including historical-critical research) that were not available to him and his age. In this sense, Maimonides would not have wanted us to be literal "Maimonideans"; he would have wanted us to imitate him more than follow him. At a time when it is fashionable for many intellectuals to dismiss the existence of truth altogether, Maimonides encourages us to search for truth, which is to search for God. His faith, both religious and philosophic, inspires us to believe with him that God has put us in this world for nothing less.

Thomas Aquinas: A Doctor for the Ages

ROMANUS CESSARIO

WHY SHOULD A MEDIEVAL Catholic priest merit a place among the most important figures of the second millennium? In part because more than seven centuries after his death his writings and teachings still seem fresh and — more importantly — true. His genius as a thinker and teacher has led thousands of scholars to carry on the intellectual projects and hand on the teachings in philosophy and theology of this thirteenth-century Neapolitan Dominican friar, whose physical size and taciturn spirit prompted some of his youthful confreres to label him the "Dumb Ox." But you don't have to be a Thomist to appreciate the genius of Thomas Aquinas (1224/5-1274). This *Doctor communis* has something to offer everyone who is serious about searching for the truth. He is a Doctor for the ages.

I

Thomas Aquinas was born to a landed aristocratic family that played a conspicuous role in the turbulent political life of the early thirteenth-century Italian peninsula. But unlike Augustine of Hippo, also a foundational doctor of the Western Church, Thomas d'Aquino, notwithstanding his prolific writing, surrenders very few details of his own biography, and so our knowledge of his family interactions and other personal matters remains limited, almost all coming secondhand, mostly from hagiographers. At the same time, the saint's theological and philosophical compositions disclose both his own spirit as a Christian believer and the magnitude of his intellectual acumen.

Aquinas was born and spent his early years in the Kingdom of Sicily. It was a time when Frederick II (1194-1250) and Pope Gregory IX (c. 1148-1241) were at warring odds with one another. In 1239, when Aquinas was fourteen, the Pope excommunicated Frederick, who had initiated an invasion into the Papal States as part of a long-delayed offensive against the Lombard communes. This momentous clash between civil and ecclesiastical authority was only the first of many conflicts that would dominate the social circumstances in which Aquinas constructed his massive corpus of theological and philosophical writings. Later at Paris, new conflicts, on the one hand between churchmen and religious orders and on the other between Aristotelian philosophers and Augustinian theologians, again provided both background and stimulus for Aquinas's intellectual work. And later still in Italy, long-standing antagonisms between the See of Rome and the churches of the East — aggravated by a then two-hundred-year-old schism — significantly influenced the way that Aquinas would deploy his intellectual energies. Even towards the end of his life, Aquinas was compelled to confront conflictual circumstances, but this time they took the form of intramural squabbles among his fellow Dominicans, some of whom still thought that ordained ministry could best be learned after the fashion of a guild-craft, while others, inspired by Aquinas's own example, understood that the Christian priest, because he participates in Christ's own mediation, requires a scientific instruction in the deposit of saving truth.

The political conflicts that affected Aquinas's personal background resulted, for the most part, from the growth and strengthening of centralizing tendencies in both ecclesiastical and secular affairs that took place at the beginning of the thirteenth century. The unprecedented expression of political as well as of theological unity in the Church achieved by Pope Innocent III at the Fourth Lateran Council in 1215 inaugurated this period of profound cultural change. Alasdair MacIntyre argues that these conditions exercised an influence even on Aquinas's treatment of such speculative concepts as natural law. Certainly, one cannot appreciate fully the kind of stability that Aquinas's theology and philosophical investigations introduced into the world of Christian thought without bearing in mind the turbulence that marked the social, political, and ecclesiastical milieus during his lifetime.

The social changes occasioned by the transition from feudal to urban Europe formed the background for the scholastic revival of the thirteenth century. Contrary to some accounts, European culture before the sixteenth-century renaissance was not darkly glum. In fact, Christian civilization in the West underwent an extraordinary renaissance in the twelfth century, when a massive effort was mounted to retrieve and organize past learning in diverse fields. This development enabled Aquinas to make creative use of the many philosophical advances that accompanied the introduction of Aristotle to the West.

During his education with the Benedictine monks at Monte Cassino and later in Naples at the first European university to operate under entirely secular control (which Frederick II founded in 1224), the young Thomas Aquinas enjoyed the usual prerogatives of his social class and standing. It seems that his parents had plans for their son to pursue an ecclesiastical career of distinction. The direction of his life changed dramatically, therefore, when he abandoned his family's aspirations and joined the newly established brotherhood of Dominicans. The traditional accounts of his attempt to join the friars, which include tales of imprisonment and attempted seduction, reflect the emotional conflict that Aquinas's decision created within his family.

Studies in Paris and Cologne followed. In these high centers of intellectual life, Aquinas joined other young Dominicans who had been placed under the tutelage of Albertus Magnus, the early Dominican theologian and natural philosopher. His education was not only traditional, involving close studies of the Scriptures, of the Western Fathers, and of Church law, but also innovative, inasmuch as Aquinas discovered the new wave of Aristotelian philosophy, which included the areas of natural, moral, and "rational" (rhetoric, grammar, and logic) philosophy.

Between 1252 and 1259, Aquinas fulfilled with signal success the obligations of a thirteenth-century university instructor and professor, notwithstanding the conflicts and disputes that continued both within and outside the lecture halls. On one occasion, the French king had to station the royal archers around the Dominican convent in Paris to defend the friars against attacks from partisans of the secular masters. These secular clerics (*secular* meaning not a member of a religious order) found it difficult to accept the new friars into their ranks. In the midst of this turmoil, Aquinas had to meet rapid changes in theology and became adept at navigating the intellectually challenging waters of the medieval scholastic *disputatio*. On August 15, 1257, both he and the Franciscan doctor Bonaventure were admitted to the *consortium magistrorum,* that is, they were recognized as full members of the professorial corps.

In 1259 Aquinas returned to the Italian peninsula, where he accomplished a variety of tasks in service to both the papacy and the Dominican Order. These tasks included preaching sermons not only to the papal household, but also to the inhabitants of the cities where the pope was residing. Today at Orvieto one can still see an outdoor pulpit that Aquinas mounted to preach the Word of God and still read sermons Aquinas preached in his native Neapolitan dialect. In the midst of duties as theological advisor for the papal curia, he also found time to teach theology to young Dominicans. The *Summa Theologiae* dates from this period. This systematic tract was intended to cultivate the preacher's ability first to ponder and then to communicate the gospel, and so served as a tool to fulfill the Dominican ideal: To contemplate and to give to others the fruits of one's contemplation.

Circumstances of conflict, however, once more directed the development of Aquinas's apostolic activity, bringing him back to Paris for a second period of teaching between 1268 and 1272. There he devoted his energies to allaying the uneasiness that the pagan philosophy of Aristotle caused among theologians of a more traditional Augustinian persuasion, while at the same time he critically engaged those who used philosophy to contradict the truths of Christianity. Thinking about the faith is always risky business. Some people are frightened by the prospect, and so fall back into a kind of credulous fideism that explains Christian doctrine by appeal only to the categories one finds in revelation itself. Others become intoxicated with the project, and so construct a kind of censorious rationalism that trims the supernatural content of divine revelation in order to fit the categories established by human reason. Aquinas's merit is that he succumbs to neither temptation.

During his second Parisian stay, Aquinas continued his battle in defense of the mendicant religious orders, in particular the Franciscans and Dominicans, whose newly authorized place within the university structure continued to cause tensions among the already-established secular masters. Before the advent of the mendicant orders, religious priests were for the large part found only in monasteries, and so avoided day-to-day involvement in Church affairs. Francis and Dominic brought the monastery to the cities and towns of Europe, and so intruded into an arena that up to that time had been dominated by a diocesan bishop and his clergy. Feelings ran high. We know of only two times in his life when Aquinas lost his composure, and one occurred when he learned that certain persons were cornering prospective students in the back streets of Paris in order to dissuade them from attending the lectures of the mendicant masters.

After the three-year cycle of lectures and disputations that constituted in the thirteenth century a term of office for the friar who held the Dominican chair at the University of Paris, Aquinas returned once again to Italy. At Naples, he took up his academic work, teaching Dominicans about the Bible and continuing to write his *Summa Theologiae*. But providence was about to intervene in a dramatic way.

During his first sojourn in the Papal States, Aquinas had composed a compendium of arguments to be used by the theologians charged by the Pope with carrying on dialogue with schismatic Byzantine theologians. So when Gregory X convoked a council at Lyons for May 1, 1274, in order to achieve mutual understanding with the separated Greeks, he numbered Aquinas among the experts who were asked to join the deliberations. While traveling northward from Naples, Aquinas suddenly fell ill, and on March 7 he died in the early hours of the morning at the Cistercian monastery of Fossanova.

Faithful to his profession of mendicant simplicity and to the Dominican objective of preaching sacred truth, Aquinas, during the course of his adult career, politely but firmly refused both the abbacy of Monte Cassino and the archbishopric of Naples. The first he declined at the start of his ministry, the second at its end. By these decisions, he disengaged himself from parochial conflicts, and so was free to make a permanent contribution to theological learning in the universal Church.

What is that permanent contribution? In his 1988 Gifford Lectures, Alasdair MacIntyre explained that Aquinas's approach to theology provides a standpoint that is coherent, comprehensive, and resourceful in its ability to deal critically and creatively with opposing views. This is not to say that Aquinas supplies the software that fits all hardware. Diversity marks his legacy. From the years following his death until the late fifteenth century, the label of "Thomist" was generally applied to those who emphasized the created world, instead of the divine ideas, as the foundation for acquiring knowledge. The ecclesiastical condemnations of Aquinas's teaching in 1277 and 1284, even though moot long before their formal revocation shortly after Aquinas's canonization in 1323, reveal the kinds of difficulties that attended a transition to the new theological forms that

Aquinas's teaching embodied. The censures, to be sure, were politically motivated, but they reveal a traditional preference for the heritage of Bernard of Clairvaux over that of Anselm of Canterbury. In brief, commentary was safe, whereas thinking was risky. Some refer to this period as "first Thomism," when the opposition to Thomist propositions arose mainly from tradition-bound theologians who were persuaded that in the end it was a mistake for a theologian to take nature too seriously.

The diverse ways that theologians explained both the origin of human knowledge and the ground for the certitude of that knowledge illustrates the kind of issues that marked this transition. At the beginning of the thirteenth century, the received tradition explained human knowledge by appeal to some variety of divine illumination. In short, God infused into the human mind whatever was required to acquire true knowledge. Illuminationists generally conceived of the soul as a mirror or receptacle ready to capture the rays of intelligibility from the Divine Mind. While such a view enjoyed the advantage of placing human intelligence into a fixed and comfortable relation with the Supreme intelligence, it also asserted that only divine illumination guaranteed that the human being obtained true and trustworthy knowledge of sensible realities.

As a result of reading Aristotle, Aquinas had come to a different conclusion about achieving certitude in knowing. Rather than looking to illumination in order to guarantee the authenticity of the created world, he argued that the created world itself, the world of mobile nature and natural things, possessed its own intelligibility and, furthermore, that God had equipped the human mind to capture it. What is more important, he argued that since human beings know the reality of the world, they also can move demonstratively from this sure knowledge back to a sure knowledge of God, at least as he is the cause of this creation. Aquinas pointed out at least five different ways in which this argument could proceed. In sum, Aquinas took away the skyhooks, and the theological world did not collapse. The problem is a perennial one, and there are still theologians who look for ways to put the skyhooks back up. In any event, it took time for some of his contemporaries to accept Aquinas's innovations in theological argument, and this explains the controversies that erupted after his death.

By the time of the sixteenth-century Protestant reform, work on Aquinas had become more identified with straightforwardly theological issues, as exemplified in the influence that his *Summa Theologiae* exercised on the Council of Trent. Those who criticized the "Common Doctor" did so because they considered either his theology not sufficiently humanist or his humanism not fully radicalized. This "second Thomism" continued to flourish widely during the early modern period. Witness that during the second half of the seventeenth century, for example, two Chinese translations of the *Summa* were published in Peking.

In the decades after the European revolutions of the late eighteenth and early nineteenth centuries, the Church again turned to Aquinas's works to solve problems mainly of a philosophical nature. This "third Thomism" is more commonly known as "neo-Thomism." Some post–Vatican II theologians, it is true, supposed that neo-Thomism signaled Thomism's last breath, but John Paul II has recently offered another assessment. Speaking of Aquinas, the Pope says, "In him, the Church's Magisterium has seen and recognized the passion for truth; and, precisely because it stays consistently within the horizon of universal, objective, and transcendent truth, his thought scales 'heights unthinkable to human intelligence'" (*Fides et Ratio,* no. 44).

II

The teaching of Thomas Aquinas has exercised an active influence mainly but by no means exclusively on Western intellectual movements for three-quarters of the millennium that is now coming to a close. The legacy of Aquinas to world culture flows like a winding river through many different terrains, while its waters pick up sediments from the different geological formations that form its bed. During its more than seven-hundred-year history, Thomism has influenced nearly every field of human learning, and Thomists have found themselves geographically dispersed, albeit unevenly, throughout the whole world.

Interest in Aquinas spread quickly after his death. Since the new mendicant orders sent their students to learn theology in places such as Paris and Oxford, Aquinas's works were first studied principally in the university cities of Europe. The earliest Thomists gathered around these new centers of learning as well as those at Cologne, Bologna, and of course Naples. The study of Aquinas then followed the development of the universities in Italy, Spain, Portugal, Germany, Bohemia, Vienna, Cracow, and Louvain. In the period before the Council of Trent and during its sessions, the major Thomists worked in Southern France and in Northern Italy, whereas in the post-Tridentine period, Aquinas's legacy flourished principally in Spain and the Spanish Netherlands. It was not until 1611, when Spanish Dominicans established a university in Manila, that Aquinas's works spread to the New World, and from there even to the Far East. In the twentieth century, Aquinas flourished in both Europe and the United States, and even rekindled Asian Thomism in authors such as the Japanese Yoshinori Inagaki.

Aquinas's legacy is not only found everywhere, but also has had an impact on every branch of higher learning. In the decades immediately following Aquinas's death, Thomists continued to welcome the introduction of Aristotle into the West, and so challenged many theological truisms. Later, in the sixteenth century, Thomists answered the objections raised by the Protestant reformers against the Church's teaching on justification, the sacraments, and the nature of the Church herself, while others were developing the theoretical groundwork for contemporary international law. From the start, then, Aquinas inspired discussions that range from mystical theology to cosmology, and from political theory to personal morality. Those who followed him, whatever their differences, shared the basic conviction that to think and teach and write *ad mentem S. Thomae Aquinatis* remains a sure guide to the truth of the Christian faith and of the human person. That influence extends to our time: It would be impossible to understand the debates and documents of the Second Vatican Council without acquaintance with the principal theses that discussions influenced by Aquinas had developed over the course of nearly seven centuries.

We learn something important about both theology and philosophy from this wide-ranging legacy. On the one hand, we learn what makes theology to be just that, a "word about God." On the other, we learn that philosophy draws the human spirit up toward "heights unthinkable to human reason."

Aquinas proceeded on the supposition that all theological writing ought to express the unity of divine truth; in his phrase, theology is like an impression of the divine knowledge in the created mind. Because he grasped this connection, Aquinas would reject today's tendency to regard theology as a constellation of diverse fields of specialized inquiry whose only unity derives from the fact that they somehow coalesce to promote Christian service. Instead he held theology to be a single divine science about God, which is able to express the one divine knowledge that governs without qualification everything that exists. In other words, Aquinas was persuaded that the best theology reflects the simplicity of God whose knowledge of himself remains the one source of all true wisdom.

Aquinas's own compositions do not fit easily the modern categories that theologians use to classify and describe their work. He was, in those terms, neither a researcher nor a theorist. On the contrary, Aquinas appreciated the unity of truth that flows from the divine simplicity, and would have been deeply repelled by conflicting truth claims produced by theologians asserting expertise in one or another theological discipline. At the same time, because Aquinas understood that theology is about ordering truths to the one Truth, and not assembling facts about many different topics, none of his works fits the literary genre of the encyclopedia, which always depends on recent research to modify what until that moment had been provisionally considered as true. Put differently, Aquinas recognized the formal difference that distinguishes theology as a divine science from religious studies as a human one. The latter always remains bound by the limits that reliance on a purely rational form of inquiry imposes. By sharp contrast, the theologian is possessed of something more.

A particular conception of the unity of theology did not keep Aquinas from developing a proficiency in diverse forms of theological and philosophical composition. Not counting his earlier expositions of certain Old Testament books — Isaiah, Jeremiah, and Lamentations — which he composed while studying with Albertus Magnus in Cologne, Aquinas produced during his relatively brief professional career (1252-1273) a body of literature that includes works of every description: theological syntheses, disputed questions, biblical commentaries, commentaries on Aristotle, commentaries on other classical works commonly in use at medieval universities, polemical writings, treatises on specific subjects, letters and replies to requests for expert opinions on particular issues, liturgical works, sermons, and prayers. All in all, a rich array of publications for one thirteenth-century man to produce within a period of little over twenty years, even taking into account the fact that he was at times aided by as many as four secretaries. Of course, Aquinas himself would not have agreed. Toward the end of his life he compared everything that he had written to straw, and like St. Paul he preferred above all things to know the Lord Jesus, who, according to the received account, himself spoke to Thomas from a crucifix hanging in the St. Nicholas chapel: "You have written well of me, Thomas! What do you desire?" To which, Thomas replied, *"Non nisi te, Domine."* Only you, Lord Jesus. Because his own "words about God" drew

Aquinas back to God, the Church sees in this Dominican the model of a true theologian.

At the same time, we can learn from Aquinas's legacy about the importance of philosophy for undertaking theological investigation. In the early part of the present century, when the revival of interest in Aquinas inaugurated by Pope Leo XIII was reaching its full vigor, certain ecclesiastical authorities decided that it would be useful to express Aquinas's philosophical principles in the form of short theses or propositions. Although this objective, undertaken in the aftermath of the Modernist crisis, aimed more toward promoting a sound pedagogy than creating a narrow ideology, the Church did give quasi-official recognition to *The Twenty-Four Theses* that were held to embody the essentials of realist philosophy to be found in Aquinas's writings.

We can indicate only some of the principal positions this effort promoted. The Thomist philosopher is best described as a metaphysical realist, who judges the conclusions, at least in their classical expression, of both idealism and positivism as untenable. The latter denies the existence of universal ideas, at least in the mind of creatures, whereas the former rejects the epistemological principle that nothing exists in the intellect that was not first in sense knowledge. In natural philosophy, Thomists defend the realism of creation, or what some theologians might want to designate the scandal of creation. In natural theology, Thomists hold the conviction that from the visible things of the universe the human mind can know the existence of God, who enjoys his own subsistent fullness of pure actual being, and who possesses no limitation of any kind, because nothing of potential remains in him. No creature enjoys this status of pure act, and so Thomists espouse in metaphysics what Father James Weisheipl calls the "disturbing distinction" between essence and existence, which entails by way of corollary the conviction that every creature depends on the actuality of borrowed existence. Thomists think only in terms of analogical predication, such that the metaphysical concept of being is analogically, not univocally, said of God, substances, and accidents. In moral philosophy, they also argue for the primacy of intelligence in determining what is true about the moral life. While some Thomists espouse other theses in philosophy, this brief catalogue of philosophical views illustrates those held by any thinker who claims to stand in historical continuity with the teachings of Thomas Aquinas.

We can understand the Holy See's decision to promote the philosophical standpoint of Aquinas by reference to the traditional way of depicting the 1879 encyclical of Pope Leo XIII, *Aeterni Patris:* "On the Restoration in Catholic Schools of Christian Philosophy According to the Mind of the Angelic Doctor Saint Thomas Aquinas." The encyclical itself does not carry this title, but Pope Leo described it in that way the following year when he declared Saint Thomas to be the patron of studies in Catholic schools.

The reference to "Christian Philosophy" recalls that neo-Thomism, as it would later become known, was promoted by the Church in response to the widespread use of Cartesian manuals of philosophy in Christian education. Seminary training was especially affected, and this realization generated well-grounded fears that a new generation of priests would find themselves not only unfamiliar with the integrity of Catholic faith but also tempted to separate truth from experience. Rationalism does not prepare the mind to believe that God sent his Son into the world to be its way, truth, and life. Recall that Aquinas, as Pope John Paul II has confirmed, produced a philosophy of "what is," not of "what seems to be." Reality offers much more to philosophize about than do appearances. Pope Leo wanted to steer Church thinking away from the fascination with the apparent that had captivated European thought in the modern period, and we can see in retrospect that his initiative promoted a flowering of Catholic intellectual life.

Aquinas inspired much of the theology and philosophy that flourished in Catholic circles during the period between the two World Wars, and his teaching continued to receive papal endorsements after the Second Vatican Council. Pope Paul VI used the ceremonies that marked the seventh centenary of the death of Saint Thomas in 1974 to commend an "authentic fidelity to Thomas." The 1983 revision of the Code of Canon Law further applauds Aquinas as a master who can lead students of theology to a deep penetration of the mysteries of salvation (CIC 252 §3). A few years earlier, the same theme had appeared in the 1979 Apostolic Constitution *Sapientia Christiana* (especially Nos. 71 & 80), which presently governs the administration of ecclesiastical universities and faculties. Finally, the 1998 encyclical letter of John Paul II restates the confidence that the Church places in Aquinas as a thinker capable of leading people to a knowledge of the truth. Although *Fides et Ratio* enforces no allegiance to a specific set of philosophical theses, it does condemn those intellectual positions that faithful adherence to Aquinas inhibits: eclecticism, historicism, scientism, pragmatism, and nihilism.

In *Fides et Ratio* the Pope also acknowledged the enduring originality of Aquinas's approach both to thinking about the truth that God has revealed in Christ and to expressing the harmonies that arise once the rational creature is enabled to ponder what "eye hath not seen" (Isaiah 64:4). What is perhaps more pertinent for earning recognition in the second millennium, the Pope also cited St. Thomas "because of the dialogue which he initiated with the Arab and Jewish thought of his time" (no. 43). Whatever its source, Aquinas, we are told, revered the truth. No wonder popes have reserved for him the distinguished epithet, "apostle of the truth."

It is Aquinas's profound love for the Incarnation that makes him still a faithful guide for preserving the Christian Church from errors that erode her confession of the gospel of Jesus Christ. Aquinas knew that because God chose to save the human race by sending his only Son in the likeness of sinful flesh, the Church of Christ is committed to reconciling the human and divine. Aquinas teaches us the right way to view the creation of the world with the new creation of the gospel. There is every reason, therefore, to suppose that at the end of the millennium about to commence he will still rank among the figures who have most influenced the course of human intellectual activity. The desire to know the truth that God has placed in the human heart will not disappear, nor will the two wings of faith and reason on which the human spirit rises to the contemplation of this truth. Thomas Aquinas illumines the dynamics of this upward flight.

Dante: A Party of One

ROBERT HOLLANDER

RARELY HAS A WRITER LEFT a more indelible mark — and under less favoring circumstances — than Dante Alighieri (1265-1321). His major work is considered one of the crowning achievements of human expression. It lives even today, nearly seven hundred years after its making, as one of the two or three greatest poems ever written. Its author was born in Florence into a family of minor nobility, Guelph in its political alignment and thus siding with the popes in the city's political tensions (as opposed to Ghibellines, at the time mainly banished from Florence, who favored the imperial cause). The struggle between the two largest political forces in medieval Europe (a struggle delineated in Robert Louis Wilken's essay on Gregory VII, the first chapter in this book) had not abated in Dante's time.

Dante was significantly involved in politics, eventually holding office as one of Florence's six Priors in 1300. Within a year, perhaps after an encounter with Pope Boniface VIII in 1301 — Dante may have been part of a political mission to the Holy See — he was sent into exile when an opposing Guelph faction in Florence took over the city. Refusing the humiliating compromises offered by his enemies, Dante saw his exile eventually become permanent. After 1302 he never again entered his native city, at that time one of the most wealthy, beautiful, and important urban centers in the Western world. The exile was a difficult period, and we know little of his itinerary around northern Italy during the last twenty years of his life. He enjoyed two lengthy sojourns at the court of the Scaligeri, in Verona (ca. 1303-1306 and 1312-1318). Upon his return from a political mission to Venice on behalf of that city's ruler, he died in Ravenna of malarial fever in September 1321.

If his life seems fairly unremarkable except for the bitterness of the exile and of his unfulfilled political hopes, it resulted in an overpowering single work, the *Comedy* (which was not known as *The Divine Comedy* until 1555, an apt editorial intervention that has remained with the poem to this day). His earlier literary activity is also of considerable interest. Perhaps as early as 1293 he had composed a work called *Vita nuova* ("New Life"), in which he assembled thirty-one poems written during the previous ten years, many of which celebrated a woman named Beatrice. There is still some debate as to the actuality of this "relationship," which in the telling seems to have been totally devoid of sexual concourse, no matter how defined. Suffice it to say that the pretext of the work is that the miraculous woman it celebrates was a flesh-and-blood Florentine woman. What is most remarkable about *Vita nuova* is that it contrives, in ways that remain securely on the side of calculated understatement, to make the reader understand that Dante's lady is to be understood as directly, and miraculously, related to the physical and noumenal presence of Christ. Beatrice is a "nine," he once explains, because the root of nine is three and that is the number of the Holy Trinity. While the poems themselves may on occasion hint at this equation, the prose, which controls them and our understanding of them, eventually serves to release a secret: loving Beatrice was his way of finding Christ in his "new life" (a phrase that can hardly fail to bring to mind Paul's frequent insistence on our conversion from the old way of being to the new). The figure of Beatrice was probably derived indirectly from the life of St. Francis, who was thought to have offered his followers as close an approximation of an experience of the nearness of Jesus as anyone since apostolic times had ever felt.

Vita nuova is the first work in the history of Western writing to take the form of commentary on one's own poems. In Dante's startling decision to frame the work in this manner, we find the demon of experiment that always drove him. Indeed, *De vulgari Eloquentia* (Concerning Eloquence in the Vernacular), one of the two succeeding unfinished works that he began while in exile, begins by claiming, rather presumptuously but altogether accurately, that no one had ever before written about the rules governing writing in the vernacular. It was written in Latin, but argued that vernacular poetry, which had only begun in Italy 150 years before with the poems of St. Francis, was worthy of all the consideration previously bestowed on Latin alone. This polemical analysis was in Latin because Dante knew that to beat those who exalted Latin, and scorned all who wrote in the "vulgar" Italian, he had to join them — at least when composing a work on such a subject.

At about the same time (ca. 1304-1307) Dante also completed the first four books of what was to have been a fifteen-book encyclopedic treatise, written in the vernacular, on the nature of philosophizing. Called *Il Convivio* ("The Banquet"), it takes the *Consolation of Philosophy of Boethius* as its model. Although at the conclusion of *Vita nuova* Dante had promised to write still more about Beatrice, in Convivio he has a new and "allegorical" beloved, the Lady Philosophy.

Convivio, like *Vita nuova*, is cast in the form of commentary on poems by its author. The poems in this case were *canzoni*, or odes, long lyrics of considerable artifice, which in *De vulgari Eloquentia* Dante claimed to be the highest possible literary form in the vernacular, lofty ("tragic" is Dante's word for this) and serious. The fifteen "treatises" *(trattati)* of the work, after an introductory treatise that was to function as introduction to the whole, were each to comment on a *canzone*. The first two of the three succeeding treatises that Dante completed deal with his new love, Philosophy. Dante says that he sought "silver" (consolation) after the death of Beatrice but found "gold" instead in the counsels of philosophy, a "lady" better suited to the more mature man that he now was. These two unfinished works both contravene *Vita nuova*'s celebration of Beatrice as the most valuable teacher of a fully charitable love that the writer could know. It is thus understandable that the *Comedy,* which presents Beatrice as giving essential meaning to Dante's life and work, in turn contradicts things said in the two abandoned texts, while essentially presenting *Vita nuova* as a necessary and praiseworthy beginning.

The fourth and last treatise of *Convivio* that Dante completed moves in more political directions. Although a Guelph by family ties, early disposition, and Florentine political allegiances, Dante in this treatise turns in the direction of empire. He addresses the question of Rome and its authority as imperial seat. The question is presented as part of a larger discussion on the nature of philosophical and imperial authority, yet it is clear that the imperial part of the argument is not necessary to its main thrust, as a result standing out all the more. This matter will resurface in the first and second cantos of *Inferno,* where state and church are seen as equally important, and then as the central concern of his later essay, *Monarchia.*

Monarchia is one of Dante's few forays into explicitly political concerns. Written in Latin to guarantee the readership of the "cultural elite" he intends to engage, probably around 1317, it offers a ringing attack upon the hierocratic position so urgently put forward by many after Pope Gregory VII. According to Dante, God created Rome to be the imperial leader of the secular world. Dante's concept of "monarchy" (synonymous with "empire") as a current possibility, however, exists only as an ideal. Except for its Roman model, it refers to few precise past and no existing temporal states, but to the divinely sanctioned secular government of all Europe that should be the essential ordering force of human affairs in this world.

Its status as ideal rather than actual, however, hardly dampens Dante's enthusiasm for the concept. The three questions that he addresses are as follows: (1) Is monarchy necessary to the well-being of the world? (2) Did the Roman people take on the office of the monarch by right? (3) Does the monarch's authority derive immediately from God or from some (mediating) minister or vicar? The "correct" answers, over against defenders of the pope's absolute authority, are "Yes," "Yes," and "Immediately from God." Of all Dante's works, this one got him into the deepest difficulty with the Church. In its own day, or shortly thereafter, it incurred the wrath of the Dominican Guido Vernani, who, in 1327, wrote a vitriolic but essentially convincing attack *(De reprobatione Monarchiae)* on its logical procedures. *Monarchia* was burned in public at least once, in 1329. It was placed on the Index in 1554, and remained prohibited until 1881.

Dante's politics in *Monarchia,* it is important to note, are more based in theology than one might expect. For him, Rome under Caesar Augustus, at the "fullness of time" when Christ chose to be born, was given the task of guiding all temporal efforts. It was thus a "universal monarchy." Dante seems to have envisioned a revived empire coming in a second "fullness of time" before the Second Coming, in which the empire would again come to rule Europe, as it had done properly only once after the era of the Caesars, under Charlemagne. This millenarian view, never stated bluntly but informing the entire work (and the *Comedy,* too, in the eyes of this reader), is completely unauthorized by Church teaching, yet it was central to Dante's political vision. The empire is God's creation, but is totally independent of the papacy, and owes the pope no fealty except (and the exception is significant) in matters of the emperor's own salvation.

This is not to say that Dante wanted to regress to the situation that preceded Gregory or to roll back Gregory's reforms. In the eleventh century Dante would probably have been almost as incensed about imperial intervention in the affairs of the Church — at least in the abstract — as he was in the fourteenth about papal intervention in affairs of state. Dante, for all his urgent attacks on papal prerogatives, did not want to see the papacy leave Italy. The *Comedy* contains vibrant calls for the papacy to return to Rome from Avignon, where Clement V had moved it in 1305. Had Dante been as anti-papal as some maintain, he would never have voiced such sentiment. He was, after all, not a Protestant, not even *avant la lettre,* as some would style him. At the end of *Monarchia,* Dante admits that the prince is in some respect subject to the pontiff, since earthly happiness is in some way *(quodammodo)* ordered toward immortal happiness. This is less a retraction than a necessary concluding gesture, aligning the responsibilities of the two great institutions.

Dante's political thought had moved from an early Guelph allegiance, reflecting the views of his intimates, to an essentially Ghibelline one. Yet his belief in the empire was always under the aegis of his belief in God. It is no accident that perhaps the chief representative of the Ghibellines in the *Comedy* is Farinata degli Uberti, whom we meet in the company of other heretics in *Inferno* X. For Dante, Ghibellinism without God promises the certain spiritual failure of those who give themselves to the political world too enthusiastically. For him, the temptation of that world was always controlled by his Christian faith — or so he would often suggest. Such a political view found few to share it. And thus, as he puts it in his own ancestor's words, he became a *"parte per te stesso"* (a party of yourself alone) [*Par.* XVII, 69].

It is important in this respect to note the dangers of taking the *Comedy* as a sort of summa of medieval thought. While one cannot deny that it at least appears to engage almost every subject that seized the imagination of the day, it is also true that to take Dante as *the* voice of late medieval Christendom is to fail to observe his heterodoxy and, one should add, his genius. Perhaps Dante's strategic advantage lay in his ability to be completely himself, unworried should he oppose generally held beliefs, while also presenting his own ideas as though they were normative. A reader of the *Comedy* unversed in medieval debates and unaware of Dante's idiosyncratic notions about them is easily persuaded that this work indeed represents the late middle ages *in nuce.* In fact, Dante finds something to quarrel with in the positions put forward by almost every recognized authority, even those he respects the most, from Aristotle (whom he honors perhaps more than any other thinker) to Aquinas (with whom he fights mainly friendly but nonetheless frequent little battles).

The *Comedy* was probably composed between 1307 and 1321. We can only begin to imagine how its germinal idea was conceived. It probably took no more than an instant for Cervantes to have the simple, fruitful idea that produced *Don Quixote*: take a middle-aged, down-at-the-heels landowner, fill his brain with the entire tradition of chivalric romance, and then have him ride forth into the world as a knight errant. In the case of Dante's *Comedy*, we likely read the result of a similar sudden inspiration, one based on a perhaps even less promising pretext: take a not-very-successful (though respected), soon-to-be-exiled civic leader and poet, and send him off to the afterworld for a week.

We shall never know what brought the work to life in Dante's mind, his first awareness of a plan. But we can see how largely the *Comedy* departs from his previous work, despite its thematic and stylistic links to his literary past. *Vita nuova, De vulgari Eloquentia,* and *Convivio* all put prose to the service of controlling and explaining verse. The *Comedy* sticks to verse. And almost everything about it is new.

To begin with, the *Comedy's* verse form *(terza rima)* is an innovation. "Loosing and binding," in the words of Erich Auerbach, its rhyme scheme (aba bcb cdc . . . yzyz) is ideal for propelling a rhymed narrative. No one had written in the form before Dante. Perhaps surprisingly, no later writers of epic in Italian (e.g., Boiardo, Ariosto, Tasso) would follow him.

Dante calls each of the one hundred divisions of the work a "canto," or "song." This word in this context is so singular and foreign that many early commentators didn't "get it," and referred to the *canti* as "chapters," a more usual and perhaps more dignified way to indicate the parts of a "serious" whole. Dante's word seems to reflect epic precedents (Virgil too was a "singer": *"Arma virumque cano,"* begins the *Aeneid*) as well as his pride in his own vernacular. In addition, the word he eventually chooses for the three large divisions of the poem, *Inferno, Purgatorio,* and *Paradiso — cantica* — had never been used for such a purpose before him. Its resonance with the Canticle of Canticles is probably not coincidental.

The choice of guide is dramatic and challenging: Virgil, the greatest of the Latin poets (for Dante and many contemporary judges). What is a pagan, damned to Limbo forever for his lack of faith, doing as guide in a Christian poem? This was a bold decision. As has frequently been pointed out, Virgil's example was seminal for many aspects of Dante's poetic strategies in the *Comedy*: to write a poem that prominently features a visit to the underworld (Dante could not read Homer's texts, though he did know of them, which explains why he can behave as though Virgil were uniquely qualified to serve as his model); that celebrates the Roman concept of political order as exemplified in the empire; and that is narrated by a poet who has been lent prophetic powers.

In addition, and perhaps most importantly, Virgil was a poet who wrote poetry as history, and Dante followed this example as well. As the work of Ulrich Leo demonstrated some years ago, Dante had been rereading the texts of Virgil and the other Latin writers of "epic" (Statius, Lucan, and Ovid) as he was finishing the fourth and last book of *Convivio*. We can say, then, that Dante chose Virgil as his guide because Virgil was his guide. Dante seems to be indicating that rereading the pagan Virgil redirected his attention to his good beginning as the Christian poet of Beatrice, the role to which he now returns in the *Comedy*.

Before Dante no one had dared to write a poem that claimed for itself revealed truth. And one can understand why. The question of the veracity of the *Comedy*'s narrative is never far from its readers' attention. In the first invocation of the poem (*Inf.* II, 7), the poet asks for the aid of the Muses (the rules of grammar and rhetoric?) and of *alto ingegno* ("lofty genius" — either, somewhat implausibly, the poet's own capacities, or, more probably but also rather disconcertingly, that of a higher Power). What follows immediately is a claim (and not an "invocation") for the ability of the poet's memory to set forth an exact record of his week-long visionary journey: *"O mente, che scrivesti ciò ch'io vidi / qui si parrà la tua nobilitate"* (O memory, that set down what I saw, here shall your worth be shown — II, 8-9). Dante here seems to acknowledge his need for two kinds of external assistance, that conferred by what one can learn about poetic discourse (figures of speech, rhetorical devices, rhymes, etc.), and that conferred by God so that the poet can conceive the meaning of his experience.

Dante's claims for the absolute veracity of the *Comedy* offend, one might say, only two classes of reader: believers and nonbelievers. In ways that would have deeply surprised and troubled St. Thomas, Dante assumed for himself the ability to write his poem using the same procedures that interpreters like Thomas believed God employed in dictating Scripture. This tactic provides one of the continuing debates in Dante criticism. To this day there is controversy over whether Dante actually wrote the "Letter to Cangrande," whose author overtly claims that he wrote the *Comedy* making use of the four senses of Scripture, almost exactly as these are defined by St. Thomas near the beginning of the *Summa* (I, i, 10). Even if Dante did not write the epistle, the techniques of signifying in the poem nevertheless centrally reflect "God's way of writing."

From Dante's first insistence that what is narrated as having occurred is to be treated as having actually occurred, it is clear he does not actually expect us to believe that the journey really took place. He does want us, though, to pay particular attention to the fact that he has claimed that it did. Here lies the central difference between the *Comedy* and more "standard" medieval allegorical visions (e.g., the *Roman de la Rose,* Brunetto Latini's *Tesoretto*). Take the moment in *Inferno* XVI when Dante stakes the credibility of his entire *comedía* on his having seen the fabulous monster Geryon. In such moments, we may sense that the poet realizes that his reader will not grant for an instant that such things really have occurred, but will recognize the reason for which the poet must make the outrageous claim. Dante does not want his poem categorized as a mere fiction, like those castigated by Aquinas and other theologians who held that poets are in effect liars and have little to say that is epistemologically valid.

In *Inferno* XXIX, Dante emphasizes this point by comparing counterfeiters, victims of a plague-like ailment in their eternal damnation, to those plague victims on the island of Aegina described by Ovid, who were replaced by "ant-people" — *"secondo che i poeti hanno per fermo"* (as the poets hold for certain). That dig in Ovid's ribs — no one will (or should) believe what a lying poet tells — is a risky and amusing joke between us and Dante. For at heart we know that his sinners, as he portrays them, are as "fictive" as Ovid's Myrmidons. Dante takes on Thomas's objections by claiming total veracity for his poem as he smilingly capitulates to them: he is, after all, only another lying poet, but one who nonetheless claims to tell "the truth," and indeed literal truth.

There are, to be sure, several moments in which he seems altogether serious about the truth claims made for his vision. Yet his careful (and often amusing) undercutting of their full impact makes the poem's readers far more comfortable than they would be were such passages not present. They allow the poem to be utterly serious when its author wants it to be (one cannot imagine such playfulness being allowed in the climactic visions of *Paradiso* XXXIII), and they allow readers to think that Dante is at least as sane as they are. Dante, while as stern a moralizing poet as one is likely to find, is a surprisingly restrained visionary.

A final example of his witty playfulness about his role as prophetic seer is worth noting. In describing the six wings adorning each of the four biblical beasts representing the authors of the Gospels in *Purgatorio* XXIX, Dante assures us that their wings were six in number (Ezekiel's cherubic creatures had only four [1:6]), that is, as many as are found in John's description of the same creatures (Revelation 4:8). Verse 105 puts this in an arresting way: *"Giovanni è meco e da lui si diparte"* (John sides with me, departing from him). No one but Dante would have made this statement in this way. "Here I follow John" would have been a more acceptable gesture for a poet to use in guaranteeing the truthfulness of his narrative. Not for Dante. Since the pretext of the poem is that he indeed saw all that he recounts as having seen, that experience, in good Thomistic procedure, is prior — he knows this by his senses. And so John is *his* witness, and not vice versa. It is an extraordinary moment.

Nothing is more difficult for one who teaches this poem to students than to convince them that all of the damned souls, no matter how attractively they present their own cases, are to be seen as justly damned. The poem creates some of its drama from the tension that exists between the narrator's view of events (in *Inferno* often represented by Virgil's interpretive remarks) and that of the protagonist. What makes our task as readers difficult is that at some pivotal moments neither the narrator nor Virgil offers clear moral judgments. Instead, Dante uses irony to undercut the alluring words of sinners who present themselves as victims rather than as perpetrators of outrage in the eyes of God. Guido da Pisa's gloss (to *Inf.* XX, 28-30) puts the matter succinctly: "But the suffering of the damned should move no one to compassion, as the Bible attests. And the reason for this is that the time for mercy is here in this world, while in the world to come there is time only for justice."

If it was John Milton's task in *Paradise Lost* to "justify the ways of God to men," Dante before him had taken on the responsibility of showing that all that is found in this world and in the next is measured by justice. Everything in God is just; only in the mortal world of sin and death do we find injustice. And it is small wonder that Dante believes there are only few living in his time who will find salvation (*Par.* XXXII, 25-27). Words for "justice" and "just" recur frequently in the poem, the noun some thirty-five times, the adjective some thirty-six. If one were asked to epitomize the central concern of the *Comedy* in a single word, "justice" might represent the best choice.

In the *Inferno* we see this insistence on God's justness from the opening lines describing Hell proper, the inscription over the gate of Hell (III, 4):

"*Giustizia mosse il mio alto fattore*" (Justice moved my maker on high). If God is just, there can be absolutely no question concerning the justness of his judgments. All who are condemned to Hell are justly condemned. Thus, when the protagonist feels pity for some of the damned, we are meant to realize that he is at fault for doing so. This is perhaps the most crucial test of us as readers that the poem offers. If we sympathize with the damned, we follow a bad example. In such a view, the protagonist's at times harsh reaction to various sinners, e.g., Filippo Argenti (canto VIII), Pope Nicholas III (canto XIX), Bocca degli Abati (canto XXXII), is not (even if it seems so to some contemporary readers) a sign of his falling into sinful attitudes himself, but proof of his righteous indignation as he learns to hate sin.

If some readers think that the protagonist is occasionally too zealous in his reactions to sinners, far more are of the opinion that his sympathetic responses to others correspond to those that we ourselves may legitimately feel. To be sure, Francesca da Rimini (canto V) is portrayed more sympathetically than Thaïs (canto XVIII), Ulysses (canto XXVI) than Mosca dei Lamberti (canto XXVIII), etc. Yet it also seems to some readers that Dante's treatment of Francesca, Ulysses, and others asks us to put the question of damnation to one side, leaving us to admire their most pleasing human traits in a moral vacuum, as it were.

It is probably better to understand that we are never authorized by the poem to embrace such a view. If we are struck by Francesca's courteous speech, we note that she is also in the habit of blaming others for her own difficulties; if we admire Farinata's magnanimity, we also note that his soul contains no room for God; if we are wrung by Pier delle Vigne's piteous narrative, we also consider that he has totally abandoned his allegiance to God for his belief in the power of his emperor; if we are moved by Brunetto Latini's devotion to his pupil, we become aware that his view of Dante's earthly mission has little of religion in it; if we are swept up in enthusiasm for the noble vigor of Ulysses, we eventually understand that he is maniacally egotistical; if we weep for Ugolino's piteous paternal feelings, we finally understand that he, too, was centrally (and damnably) concerned with himself, even at the expense of his children.

Dante's innovative but risky technique was to trust us, his readers, with the responsibility for seizing upon the details in the narratives told by these sympathetic sinners in order to condemn them on the evidence that issues from their own mouths. It was indeed, as we can see from the many readers who fail to take note of this evidence, a perilous decision for him to have made. Yet we are given at least two clear indicators of the attitude that should be ours. Twice in *Inferno* figures from Heaven descend into Hell to further God's purpose in sending Dante on his mission. Virgil tells of the coming of Beatrice to Limbo. She tells him, in no uncertain terms, that she feels nothing for the tribulations of the damned and cannot be harmed in any way by them or by the destructive agents of the place that contains them (*Inf.* II, 88-93). All she longs to do is to return to her seat in Paradise (*Inf.* II, 71). And when the angelic intercessor arrives to open the gates of Dis, slammed shut by the rebellious angels against Virgil, we are told that this benign presence has absolutely no interest in the situation of the damned or even of the living Dante. All he desires is to complete his mission and be done with such things (*Inf.* IX, 88, 100-103).

Such indicators should point us in the right direction. It is a continuing monument, both to the complexity of Dante's poem and to some readers' desire to turn it into a less morally determined text than it ultimately is, that so many of us have such difficulty wrestling with its moral implications. This is not to say that the poem is less because of its complexity, but precisely the opposite. Its greatness is reflected in its rich and full realization of the complicated nature of human behavior and of the difficulty of moral judgment for living mortals. It asks us to learn, as does the protagonist, as we proceed.

One tradition of deathbed utterance has it that Calderón's last words were, "Dante, why were you so difficult?" Whether or not the anecdote is true, the lament is a fitting one. We might choose a different version of this question: "Dante, why were you so good?" His extraordinary gifts as poet — and these are the most salient aspects of what he has left behind — enable him to reach everyone who loves to watch or hear language do everything it can do. In this he is like Homer and Shakespeare. And, like them, he enjoys some of this power even when he is translated. He has the further ability to enter the hearts of nearly everyone: "Monarchists" read him their way; "Papists," theirs.

For some conservative Catholics he is the authentic voice of the medieval Church; for many liberal atheists he is an authentic voice of human suffering and hope. Each of us reads his own Dante, and admires what he reads. How would Dante react, come back to experience it, to all our fuss over him? It seems reasonable to believe that, first of all, he would be pleased with the extraordinary amount of attention his work continues to gather. The poet who, with unbelievable boldness in *Inferno* IV, had made himself one of the six major poets between antiquity and his own day (Homer, Virgil, Horace, Ovid, Lucan, . . . Dante), now looks modest, in the world's estimation; he has eclipsed, for most readers, all but Homer.

But then do we not imagine hearing him complain, over and over, about how badly we now read him? Even posthumously he probably would consider that he had ended up what he had said he was in his political endeavors: "a party of one."

Columbus and the Beginning of the World

ROBERT ROYAL

A S ORSON WELLES FAMOUSLY REMARKED, playing the unscrupulous Harry Lime in the film *The Third Man:* "In Italy for thirty years, under the Borgias, they had warfare, terror, murder, and bloodshed, but they produced Michelangelo, Leonardo da Vinci, and the Renaissance. In Switzerland they had brotherly love. They had five hundred years of democracy and peace, and what did they produce? The cuckoo clock." Lime's history was more than a little vague and self-serving (Welles himself seems to have been titillated by this dangerous truth since he added it to Graham Greene's original script for the film). Fifteenth-century Italy in particular, and Europe more generally, drew their vitality from a lot more than Borgias and Machiavellianism. But it is a paradox of history that social turmoil often offers rich soil for human achievement.

The world we know began in the fifteenth century. Not the world of course in the sense of human life or human civilizations, which had already existed for millennia, but the world as a concrete reality in which all parts of the globe had come into contact with one another and begun to recognize themselves as part of a single human race — a process still underway. The spherical globe we had known about since the classical world; in the Middle Ages, readers of Dante took it for granted. Yet it was only because of a small expedition by a few men driven by a mishmash of personal ambition, religious motives, and the desire for profit that an old mathematical calculation was turned into a new human fact. Or as a historian sixty years later accurately characterized the discovery of the New World, it was "the greatest event since the creation of the world (excluding the incarnation and death of Him who created it)."

In our own confused way, we continue to pay homage to that achievement. In 1999, NASA will put a satellite into an orbit a little less than a million miles out into space at what is called L-1, the libration point where the gravity of the earth and the sun exactly balance one another. Equipped with a telescopic lens and video camera, it will provide a twenty-four-hour-a-day image of the surface of the earth. Not surprisingly, one of the enthusiasts behind the project is Al Gore, probably the most environmentally agitated public figure alive. But in spite of the damage that Gore and many others believe we humans have inflicted on the planet since our first large steps in exploring it, and despite the laments of multiculturalists about Europe's rise to world dominance, the new satellite will be called Triana, after Rodrigo de Triana, who first spotted lights on land from the deck of the Pinta during the first voyage of Columbus.

Perhaps the name is only a bow to growing Hispanic influence in the United States; perhaps it hints that we would like to think of ourselves as equally on the verge of another great age of discovery. But whatever our sense of the future, the Columbus discoveries and the European intellectual and religious developments that lay behind them are today at best taken for granted, at worst viewed as the beginning of a sinister Western hegemony over man and nature. The last five centuries, of course, offer the usual human spectacle of great glories mixed with grim atrocities. But we cannot evaluate the voyages of discovery properly — much less the fifteenth-century culture from which they sprang — without gratitude for what they achieved or understanding of their human dimensions. In the fifteenth century, the discoveries were rightly regarded as close to a miracle, especially given the way the century had begun.

The early 1400s were marked by profound religious, political, economic, and even environmental turmoil. At one point in the first decade of the century, there were simultaneously three claimants to the papal throne and three to the crown of the Holy Roman Empire. And the large-scale institutional crises were only a small part of the story. Europe was still suffering from the devastation wrought at the height of the Black Death over half a century earlier and in smaller waves thereafter. Overall, something like 40 percent of the population disappeared in the mid-fourteenth century, in some regions even more. Land lay fallow for lack of workers, villages were deserted, poverty spread. As many modern environmentalists have devoutly wished, nature took its vengeance as human population decreased. Wolves multiplied and returned, even appearing in capital cities. Human predators — in the form of brigands — made travel unsafe over wide areas. The consequences of the retreat of civilization spurred Henry V, fabled victor of Agincourt, to offer rewards for the elimination of both types of pests. Though the beauty of landscapes emerged as never before in contemporary painting and literature, it was not a century that indulged itself in easy sentimentality about the goodness of unimproved nature, human or otherwise. On the contrary, natural hardships spurred the fifteenth century to nearly unparalleled achievements.

But if the internal situation were not enough, Europe was also being squeezed by forces from outside. In 1453, the Ottoman Turks finally succeeded in taking Byzantium. Turkish troops had already been fighting as far into the Balkans as Belgrade a few years earlier. Otranto, in the heel of Italy, fell to them in 1480 for a time. We might have expected the Christian powers to lay aside rivalries momentarily and defend themselves from an alien culture and religion. But the main Atlantic nation-states — England, France, and Spain — were still only beginning to take shape. The rest of Western Europe was broken, despite the theoretical claims of the emperor, into a crazy quilt of competing small powers. So no coordinated effort occurred, though Pius II and other popes called for a crusade. Pius even wrote to Sultan Muhammad II, conqueror of Constantinople, inviting him to convert to Christianity. Whether this letter was intended seriously or as a mere pretext for further action, it failed. Neither "European" nor "Christian" interests were sufficiently united to galvanize the effort. The pope died in 1464 at the eastern Italian port of Ancona waiting for his people to rally behind him.

A crusade to retake the Holy Land was sometimes a mere pipe dream, sometimes a serious proposal during the course of the century. Ferdinand of Spain listened frequently to such plans, but refrained from doing much. (Machiavelli praises him in *The Prince* as one of those rulers who shrewdly take pains to appear good without necessarily being so.) Charles VIII of France invaded Italy in 1494 but also had in mind an attempt to retake Constantinople and restore the Eastern Christian Empire. Earlier, Henry V, on his way to Agincourt, proclaimed his intentions not only to assume the French throne but to "build again the walls of Jerusalem." Western Europe had a persistent if vague sense of responsibility to defend Christianity from Islamic military threats and a deeper need to recover the parts of Christendom lost to Muslim conquest, even if the good intentions were thwarted by intra-European distractions.

Had Islam continued its advance, much of Europe might have then resembled the cultures we now associate with the Middle East. The Americas might have been largely Muslim countries as opposed to largely Christian ones. Islam was more advanced than Europe in 1492, but in the paradoxical ways of culture, its very superiority contributed to its being surpassed. Muslims do not seem to have taken much interest in Western technical developments in navigation, and even well-placed countries like Morocco were never moved to brave the high seas in search of new lands. European technological innovation and military advance may have been born of necessity, given the superiority of outside cultures and the conflicts and rivalries among European nations.

This reminds us of something often overlooked in most contemporary historical surveys. The "Eurocentric" forces, of which we now hear so much criticism, were actually something quite different in the fifteenth century. What we today call "Europeans" thought of themselves as part of Christendom, and a Christendom, as we shall see, that desperately needed to return to some of its founding truths. Similarly, they did not regard themselves as the bearers of the highest culture. Ancient Greece and Rome, they knew, had lived at a higher level, which is why the Renaissance felt the need to recover and imitate classical models. The fabled wealth of the distant Orient and the clearly superior civilization of nearby Islam did not allow Christendom to think itself culturally advanced or, more significantly, to turn in on itself, as self-satisfied empires of the time such as China did. Contemporary European maps — the ones all the early mariners consulted in the Age of Discovery — bear witness to their central belief: Jerusalem, not Europe, was the center of the world.

But this very sense of threat and inferiority, combined with the unsettled social diversity of Europe at the time, gave Europeans a rich and dynamic restlessness. Not surprisingly, the rise towards a renewed Europe began in the places least affected by the population implosion and, therefore, more prosperous: what we today call the Low Countries and, above all, Northern Italy. Renaissances, as Erwin Panofsky demonstrated a few decades ago, had been occurring in Europe since the twelfth century. But the one that took place in Northern Italy in the fifteenth century — the one we call *the* Renaissance — produced multiple and wide-ranging consequences.

Pius II was in many ways emblematic of the mid-century. A cultivated humanist born in Siena in 1405 with the imposing name Aeneas Sylvius Piccolomini, he initially came under the spell of St. Bernardino, who preached a strictly observant reformed Franciscan life (of which more anon). But he shortly became attracted to the exciting life of the Renaissance Italian humanists, which is to say libertinism and literary pursuits. He shifted parties among papal contenders, pursuing his own ambitions for many years, wrote a popular history *(Historia rerum ubique gestarum)* that gathered together wide-ranging facts and fictions about foreign lands, and even became imperial poet and secretary to the Holy Roman Emperor Frederick III. But compared with the squabbling popes and anti-popes who preceded him and the colorful escapades of the Borgias, Pius had his virtues. He was learned and hard-working, enjoyed nature, sought reform, and could have made a difference in Europe had his office enjoyed the respect it once had and was to have again later. The religious renaissance, however, like the cultural, scientific, and artistic one with which we are more familiar, had to come from other sources.

Renaissance achievements found multiple and overlapping uses in a Europe in ferment. The geometry developed by the Florentine Paolo Toscanelli allowed Fillippo Brunelleschi, over the objections of a commission of Florentine experts, to dare construction of the unsupported dome that crowns the magnificent Florentine Duomo. Just a few decades later, an intellectually curious Genoese mariner corresponded with Toscanelli in preparation for his attempts to convince another panel of experts in Spain that it was possible to sail west to the Indies (no serious thinker at the time, by the way, believed the earth was flat). His figures were wrong; the distance was greater than he claimed. The experts — and perhaps Columbus himself — knew it. But it was an age when for various reasons people had the faith to attempt things beyond what was previously thought possible. It is worth looking closely at some of those reasons.

Much has recently been written, for example, claiming that the Christian dimension of Columbus's personality was merely a cover for greed and ambition. These alleged traits are then read as a metaphor for a hypocritical European expansion under the cover of religion. Hypocrites certainly existed in the fifteenth century, as they do today. But real history — as opposed to anachronistic morality tales — is always more complex than the simple motives we project back onto figures quite different from ourselves. Like the Italian humanists, who are often wrongly portrayed as modern unbelieving intellectuals, Columbus combined his faith with new knowledge and new interests. But that did not make his faith any less real. He wanted that Renaissance ideal, glory: in this case, that of an unprecedented voyage. He drove hard bargains with Ferdinand and Isabella to secure the financial benefits of his discoveries for himself and his descendants. (The Muslim conquests and consequent monopolies over Eastern trade routes made the European search for alternate routes all the more necessary and profitable.) Yet when all the mundane reasons have been listed, the spiritual dimension of the project remains in ways that are quite unexpected.

In the preface to his *Libro de las profecías* (Book of Prophecies), an anthology of prophetic texts that he compiled near the end of his life, Columbus relates to Ferdinand and Isabella how, long before he ever approached them, he had become convinced that the westward voyage was not merely possible but his own personal vocation:

> During this time, I searched out and studied all kinds of texts: geographies, histories, chronologies, philosoph[ies], and other subjects. With a hand that could be felt, the Lord opened my mind to the fact that it would be possible to sail from here to the Indies, and He opened my will to desire to accomplish this project. This was the fire that burned within me when I came to visit your Highnesses.

Of course, the reading alone suggests we are dealing with an unusual kind of sailor, one who, like the humanists of his day, has engaged in sifting and comparing ancient and modern knowledge for new purposes. There is some irony, then, in the fact that he claims that God intended to produce a *milagro ebidentísimo* ("highly visible miracle") in this enterprise by using an uneducated man: "For the execution of the journey to the Indies, I was not aided by intelligence, by mathematics, or by maps. It was simply the fulfillment of what Isaiah had prophesied."

Columbus clearly employed considerable intelligence, mathematical skill, and geographical knowledge in planning his route. He also knew from much experience at sea that winds in the Atlantic nearer the equator would carry him west, those to be found more to the north would take him east, back to Europe. And he was alert to other environmental signs. Late in the first voyage he turned south to follow a flock of birds that he rightly assumed were headed towards land. Without this chance or providential fact, he probably would have come ashore somewhere between Virginia and Florida instead of the Caribbean, with doubtless immensely different effects on subsequent world history.

Despite all the knowledge, abstract and practical, that Columbus brought to bear on his task, the religious intuitions he describes may strike us as bordering on delusion, on a par with the equally unexpected mystical speculations of the mathematician Pascal, or Newton's commentaries on the prophecies in the Book of Daniel. But anyone familiar with how prophecies have functioned throughout history knows they often work themselves out in ways their authors never envisioned. In Columbus's case, we may wish to avoid judging too quickly the "hand that could be felt" and other evidence that at times he seems to have heard something like divine locutions. They may have been delusions, intuitions, or something else moving in the depths of human history.

Far from being a later and idealized reinterpretation of his own past, Columbus's remarks are confirmed by a curious source. Recent scholars have discovered notes in Columbus's own hand dated 1481, over a decade before his first voyage, in the back of a copy of Aeneas Sylvius Piccolomini's (the later Pius II) *Historia rerum ubique gestarum*. There Columbus compiles a shorter list of prophecies from various sources which, it now seems perfectly clear, guided his whole life project.

Columbus's religious side seems to have grown out of a religious renaissance that occurred in fifteenth-century Europe. The *devotio moderna,* beginning with Gerard Groote and the Brethren of the Common Life, spread among both religious and laypeople, calling for a return to a more personal religion modeled on the evangelical virtues of the early Church. Its best-known writer was Thomas à Kempis, whose *Imitation of Christ* (ca. 1427) has influenced numerous individuals and movements, Catholic and Protestant, over the centuries. As late as the middle of the sixteenth century, Ignatius of Loyola, for example, the founder of the Jesuits, made it the first book he read when he decided to begin a serious religious life. The *devotio moderna* shaped figures as diverse as Nicholas of Cusa and Erasmus. In many ways, it paralleled the impulses behind the secular Renaissance in its living reappropriation of the religious past as the basis for the future.

Less known, however, is the Observant or Observantine current within the fifteenth century, first among the Franciscans, but later among other orders and lay groups. In fact, one of the major religious disputes for monasteries at the time was the need to choose between strict Observant and non-reformed Conventual rules. (Martin Luther began his religious life in an Observant Augustinian community.) The Franciscans numbered among their members figures like Saint Bernardino of Siena, Saint James of the Marches, and Saint John Capistrano. Their efforts, too, looked to a religious renaissance by way of return to the more austere and humble ways of early Christianity. For our present purposes, it is also necessary to note that, mixed in with that more austere life, there were occasionally garbled versions of the millennial speculations of Joachim of Fiore, a twelfth-century Cistercian abbot, for whom a new age of the Holy Spirit and the final age of the world seemed not far distant.

We have no indisputable evidence that Columbus was a third-order Franciscan Observantine, but his way of dress in his final years in Spain appears to have been similar to theirs. When he traveled through Spain, he stayed at Franciscan monasteries rather than the homes of noblemen. Uncertainties about Columbus's early history and the history of the Observants in Spain prevent any greater precision, but it is clear that, mixed in with his other motives, he early on had absorbed some of the millennial currents of his time. Specifically, he seems to have believed that one reason to open the Western route to the Orient was to enable the gospel finally to be preached to all nations, a prerequisite to the end of the world and the triumphal second coming of Christ that some Joachimites predicted would occur in the middle of the sixteenth century.

Significantly, Columbus also seems to have believed something not found in any of Joachim's writings: that Joachim had predicted that a king of Spain would liberate the Holy Land. Though Columbus had a personal reason to keep Ferdinand and Isabella interested in the enterprise of the Indies, he also often urged them to undertake a crusade. The fact that Spain reconquered the kingdom of Granada only at the beginning of 1492 gave Spaniards a sense greater than that of most other Europeans of the need to resist Muslim incursions. In less savory forms, this sense contributed to the Inquisition's injustices to Spanish Muslims and Jews, who were expelled from Spain on the very day Columbus set sail. Columbus's urgings went unheeded, but we have good evidence of his sincerity. For the last decade of his life the various wills he made altered different clauses, but one remained constant: he directed the executors of his estate to set up a fund in Genoa's Bank of Saint George to help pay for the liberation of Jerusalem. Whatever other motives we may attribute to him, there is no question that on spiritual matters he put his money where his mouth was.

Much of this real history has been obscured for a long time by persons who found it expedient to use Columbus as a symbolic figure. For most older Americans, he was presented as a heroic proto-American, combating the obscurantism of reactionary Spanish Catholics who thought he would sail off the end of the flat earth. (As we have seen, neither Columbus nor his intellectual critics believed in such absurdities.) In that reading, he became a forerunner of American Protestantism, modern science, and capitalist enterprise. It is no great loss that we have discarded that historical illusion.

Columbus also did service as an ethnic hero for Catholics, mostly Irish and Italian, during the large waves of immigration at the end of the nineteenth and beginning of the twentieth century. There was less harm here, because he was a true hero. Enthusiasm grew so heated that on the four hundredth anniversary of his voyage in 1892 efforts were made to have him canonized. But Leo XIII, fully aware of Columbus's irregular marital situation (for reasons of inheritance he never married the woman he lived with after his wife died), contented himself with praising his human virtues: "For the exploit is in itself the highest and grandest which any age has ever seen accomplished by man; and he who achieved it, for the greatness of mind and heart, can be compared to but few in the history of humanity."

In recent years, of course, Columbus's standing as hero has come under severe assault. He and the culture he represented have been castigated for initiating the modern cultural dominance of Europe and every subsequent world evil: colonialism, slavery, cultural imperialism, environmental damage, and religious bigotry. There is a kernel of truth in these charges, but obviously to equate a single individual or a complex entity like a culture with what are currently judged to be the negative dimensions of the emergence of an interconnected human world is to do great historical injustice to both individuals and ideas.

Europeans, for example, had an ambivalent stance towards the new peoples they encountered. On the one hand, there arose almost instantaneously the beginnings of the "noble savage" myth, which had a varied career in the hands of writers like Thomas More, Montaigne, and Rousseau. On the other hand, actual experience of the new cultures revealed peoples who displayed much savagery and sometimes little nobility.

Columbus himself adhered to one side or the other in this culture war at different times in his life. In one of his first communications with the Spanish monarchs after the discovery, he described the Taínos of the Caribbean in glowing terms:

I see and know that these people have no religion whatever, nor are they idolaters, but rather they are very meek and know no evil. They do not kill or capture others and are without weapons. They are so timid that a hundred of them flee from one of us, even if we are teasing. They are very trusting; they believe there is a God in Heaven, and they firmly believe that we come from Heaven. They learn very quickly any prayer we tell them to say, and they make the sign of the cross. Therefore Your Highnesses must resolve to make them Christians.

As the self-contradictions of this passage suggest, Columbus was under the spell of one current in European mythology that believed such "uncivilized" peoples to be somehow closer to the conditions of the Garden of Eden than those enmeshed in the conflicts of "civilization."

In fact, the Taínos themselves were enmeshed in the tribal raiding, slavery, and cannibalism that existed in the Caribbean long before any European arrived (the word "cannibal" is a corruption of the native term for the fierce Caribs who eventually gave their name to the whole region). Columbus was for a while on surprisingly good terms with his Taínos, who in turn used the Spaniards to their advantage against their enemies. But the distance between the cultures was great, and, with the arrival of less-than-ideal explorers in subsequent voyages, the situation took a bad turn. Towards the end of his third voyage, Columbus wrote to complain about criticism of his governorship over both natives and Spaniards:

At home they judge me as a governor sent to Sicily or to a city or two under settled government and where the laws can be fully maintained, without fear of all being lost. . . . I ought to be judged as a captain who went from Spain to the Indies to conquer a people, warlike and numerous, and with customs and beliefs very different from ours.

Columbus had discovered that the Indians were real flesh-and-blood human beings, with the same mix of good and evil that everywhere constitutes the human condition.

Today, the usual way of characterizing the behavior of the Europeans at this early stage is to fault them for not having the kind of sensitivity to the Other that a modern anthropologist or ethnologist would bring to such situations. Overlooked in this condemnation is the fact that it was precisely out of these tumultuous conflicts that the West began to learn how to understand different cultures as objectively as possible in their own terms. Columbus himself astutely noted differences between the various sub groupings of Taínos as well as their distinctiveness from other tribes. And even when he was driven to harsh action — against both Indians and Spaniards — it was not out of mere desire for power. Bartolomé de las Casas, the well-known defender of the Indians, notes the "sweetness and benignity" of the admiral's character and, even while condemning what actually occurred, remarks, "Truly I would not dare blame the admiral's intentions, for I knew him well and I know his intentions were good." Las Casas attributes Columbus's shortcomings not to malign intent but to ignorance concerning how to handle an unprecedented situation.

This raises the question of larger intentions and the world impact of fifteenth-century European culture. The atrocities committed by Spain, England, Holland, and other European powers as they spread out over the globe in ensuing centuries are clear enough. No one today defends them. Less known, however, are the currents within that culture that have led to the very universal principles by which, in retrospect, we criticize that behavior today. For instance, not only Las Casas, but a weighty array of other religious thinkers began trying to specify what European moral obligations were to the new peoples.

Las Casas, who was the bishop of Chiapas, Mexico, where relations between mostly native populations and the central government remain dicey even today, bent over backwards to understand local practices. He once even described human sacrifices as reflecting an authentic piety and said that "even if cruel [they] were meticulous, delicate, and exquisite," a view that some of his critics have remarked exhibits a certain coldness towards the victims. Other missionaries learned native languages and recorded native beliefs. The information coming from the New World stimulated Francisco de la Vitoria, a Dominican theologian at the University of Salamanca in Spain, to develop principles of natural law that, in standard histories, are rightly given credit as the origin of modern international law. To read Vitoria on the Indies is to encounter an atmosphere closer to the UN Universal Declaration of Human Rights than to sinister Eurocentrism.

Las Casas and Vitoria influenced Pope Paul III to make a remarkable statement in his 1536 encyclical *Sublimis Deus*:

Indians and all other people who may later be discovered by the Christians are by no means to be deprived of their liberty or the possession of their property, even though they be outside the faith of Jesus Christ. . . . Should the contrary happen it shall be null and of no effect. . . . By virtue of our apostolic authority we declare . . . that the said Indians and other peoples should be converted to the faith of Jesus Christ by preaching the word of God and by the example of good and holy living.

The Spanish crown itself had moral qualms about the conquest. Besides passing various laws trying to eliminate atrocities, it took a step unmatched before or since by any expanding empire: it called a halt to the process while theologians examined the question. In the middle of the sixteenth century, Charles V ordered a theological commission to debate the issue at the monastery of Valladolid. Las Casas defended the Indians. Juan Ginés de Sepúlveda, the greatest authority on Aristotle at the time, argued that Indians were slaves by nature and thus rightly subject to Spanish conquest. Though the commission never arrived at a clear vote and the Spanish settlers were soon back to their old ways, Las Casas's views were clearly superior and eventually prevailed.

Conquest aside, the question of even peaceful evangelizing remains very much with us. Today, most people, even Christians, believe it somehow improper to evangelize. The injunction to preach the gospel to all nations, so dear to Columbus's heart, seems an embarrassment, not least because of the ways the command has been misused. But some of the earlier missionaries tried a kind of inculturation that recognized what was good in the native practices and tried to build a symbolic bridge between them and the Christian faith. The Franciscans in New Spain and the Jesuits in Canada, for example, tried this approach. Not a few of them found martyrdom.

Many contemporary believers do not think that there was much need to evangelize. This usually arises out of the assumption that native religions are valid in their own way. It will not do, however, given the anthropological evidence, to make facile assumptions that all spiritual practices are on an equal plane. The early explorers who encountered them did not think so, and neither should we. For example, the Mexican novelist Carlos Fuentes, no special friend of Christianity or the Spanish conquest, in the very act of admiring the richness of Aztec culture, characterizes the Aztec gods as "a whole pantheon of fear." Fuentes deplores the way that missionaries often collaborated with unjust appropriation of native land, but on a theological level notes the epochal shift in native cultures thanks to Christian influence: "One can only imagine the astonishment of the hundreds and thousands of Indians who asked for baptism as they came to realize that they were being asked to adore a god who sacrificed himself for men instead of asking men to sacrifice themselves to gods, as the Aztec religion demanded."

This Copernican Revolution in religious thought has changed religious practice around the world since it was first proclaimed in Palestine two millennia ago, yet is all but invisible to modern critics of evangelization. Any of us, transported to the Aztec capital Tenochtitlàn or to many other places around the world before the influence of Christianity and Europe, would react the way the conquistadors did — with rage and horror. We might not feel much different about some of the ways that Europeans, imitating Islamic practice, evangelized at times by the sword and perpetrated grave injustices around the world. But it is reductionist in the extreme to regard evangelization simply as imperialism. The usual uncritical way in which we are urged to respect the values of other cultures has only the merest grain of truth buried beneath what is otherwise religious indifferentism.

For all our sense of superiority to this now half-millennium-old story, we still face some of the same questions that emerged in the fifteenth century. We still have not found an adequate way to do justice to the claims of both universal principle and particular communities. We have what Václav Havel has called a "thin veneer of global civilization" mostly consisting of CNN, Coca Cola, blue jeans, rock music, and perhaps the beginning glimmer of something approaching a global agreement on how we should treat one another and the planet.

But that minimal unity conceals deeper conflicts involving not only resistance to superficiality but the survival of particular communities of meaning. We say, for example, that we have an equal respect for all cultures — until we come up against religious castes and sexism, clitorectomies and deliberate persecution. Then we believe that universal principles may take precedence. But whose universal principles? A Malaysian prime minister has lately instructed us that, contrary to international assumptions, "Western values are Western values: Asian values are universal values." It may take another five hundred years to decide whether that is so, or whether the opposition it assumes between East and West will persist.

All of this may seem a long way from the fifteenth century. But it is not mere historical fantasy to see in that beginning some of the global issues that are now inescapably on the agenda for the new millennium. Christianity and Islam, the two major proselytizing faiths in the world, are still seeking a modus vivendi. The global culture initiated by Columbus will always be inescapably European in origin and, probably, in basic shape. We chose long ago not to stay quietly at home and build the otherwise quite wonderful contraptions called cuckoo clocks. That decision brought (and brings) many challenges, but the very struggle should remind us of the glorious and ultimately providential destiny of the ongoing global journey that began in the fifteenth century.

Calvin and the Christian Calling

ALISTER McGRATH

THE SIXTEENTH CENTURY was a period of tumultuous change in Western Europe. The need for some kind of moral and intellectual shake-up within the church had been obvious for some time. Many religious and political writers of the fifteenth century had been aware of the weaknesses of the medieval church and the society in which it was embedded. However, there are good reasons for thinking that few were really prepared for the radical events of the sixteenth century, which are generally referred to collectively as "the Reformation."

The Reformation remains of central importance for Christian theology and the life of the Christian church. As the discussion of the "Evangelicals and Catholics Together" document has made clear, the theological agenda of the Reformation remains of continuing importance to modern Christianity, particularly in the United States. The Reformation raised issues that remain live issues today — questions such as "How am I saved?" or "How do I recognize a true church?" Although modern academic theology prefers the mystical world of Baudrillard's praxis of location and the semiotics of a post-Saussurean world of self-referencing signifiers, it is clear that the issues raised by the Reformation simply will not go away. Nor should they be allowed to. They remain essential if the churches are to retain their identity as Christian bodies.

In taking a retrospective look at the second millennium, it is therefore both inevitable and entirely proper to explore the continuing impact of the Reformation, particularly concerning religion and public life. Three figures would immediately suggest themselves as candidates for discussion.

Martin Luther (1483-1546) and Huldrych Zwingli (1484-1531) represent the first phase of the Reformation, John Calvin (1509-64) the second.

It is easy to understand why the editors of *First Things* chose Calvin for their purpose. Calvin's task can be thought of as consolidation rather than initiation. The first phase of the Reformation focused on issues relating to personal salvation and the need for reform in the life of the church. Although Calvin never lost sight of these themes, he is perhaps best remembered for his detailed exposition of the leading themes of the Reformed faith in his *Institutes of the Christian Religion* — widely regarded as the most significant religious work of the sixteenth century — and his wrestling with issues concerning the identity of the church and its place in public life. This second aspect of his thinking developed against the all-important background of the life of the city of Geneva, which can be thought of as the laboratory within which Calvin forged his new ideas.

Calvin has excited a variety of responses, both from those who read him and from those who only read about him. He has been the object of much attention from theologians, church leaders, and historians. Some of that attention has been uncritical and laudatory; in that view, Calvin is the man who got (virtually) nothing wrong. For others, Calvin was the "dictator of Geneva," a personally unattractive person who got (virtually) nothing right. Neither approach is of much value in understanding the man and his legacy.

Although Calvin is widely regarded as Swiss (did he not work in Geneva?), it needs to be made clear from the outset that he was French. Born in 1509 in the city of Noyon, northeast of Paris, he was baptized as "Jehan Cauvin." His father intended his son to have a career in the church, and took what steps were necessary to secure this. At some point in the 1520s, Calvin went to the University of Paris to study arts, his intention being to proceed to study theology, where it is generally thought that he became acquainted with at least some of the leading ideas of Lutheranism. Calvin's original career plan went awry, though not on account of his personal religious views. His father appears to have become embroiled in a financial scandal at Noyon, making an ecclesiastical career problematical for Calvin. As a result, Calvin left Paris at some point between 1526 and 1528 and studied civil law at Orleans, graduating in 1531. Calvin's competence in matters of civil law would be of no small importance during his Geneva period.

Meanwhile, Paris was becoming increasingly agitated with Lutheranism. While the Faculty of Theology at the University of Paris was hostile to the new religious movement, the King of France, Francis I, was more positive. The agitation grew so great that when the rector of the university, Nicholas Cop, delivered an inaugural address in 1533 suggesting the need for reform of the church, it provoked outrage, and obliged Cop to flee for his life. It is not entirely clear why Calvin came to be associated with the address — some believed he had a hand in writing it — but in any event he too left Paris in haste. Cop sought refuge in the Swiss city of Basle where Calvin joined him in early 1535.

By this stage, Calvin appears to have accepted something of the agenda of the Reformation — Calvin scholars have spilled much ink over a tantalizingly opaque passage in one of Calvin's later writings, which speaks of his undergoing a "sudden conversion" at some unspecified date and place. Early writings, such as a privately published commentary on Seneca's *On Clemency* (1532), cast little light on his religious views. Yet while in exile in Basle, Calvin penned the first edition of a work that would establish his reputation as a vigorous and informed defender of the reformed faith. *Institutes of the Christian Religion* appeared in 1536, and would undergo successive revisions until the final edition of 1559. While it would not be fair to Calvin to suggest that this is his only work of importance, there is little doubt that it continues to be his most influential work.

Calvin's future remained uncertain. After various meanderings in Europe, he returned to Paris to settle some family affairs. In July 1536, he set out for the city of Strasbourg with the intention of pursuing a scholarly career. A war in the region forced Calvin to make a detour to the south, so as to approach Strasbourg from Geneva. He had no intention of settling there.

Geneva was a free city at the time, having won her liberty through a revolt in 1535 against the duchy of Savoy. With support from the Swiss Protestant city of Berne, the Genevans defeated Savoy's attempt to regain control, and by the summer of 1536, Geneva proclaimed itself a republic committed to the cause of the Reformation. The religious affairs of the city, although nominally under the control of the city council, were in effect directed by William Farel and Pierre Viret. Farel recognized Calvin during his brief stay in Geneva, and invited him to remain in Geneva and help consolidate the Reformation in that city.

Initially, things went well for Calvin. He played a prominent role in a disputation that led the neighboring city of Lausanne to accept the Reformation in September 1536. Elections to the city council — the supreme power within the new Genevan republic — increased the presence of councillors sympathetic to Farel and Calvin. Yet tensions erupted in 1538 over what both Farel and Calvin came to see as Geneva's excessive dependence upon Berne. In April of that year, the city council expelled both men from Geneva, prompting Calvin to move to Strasbourg.

During his period in Strasbourg, Calvin served as a pastor to a local French-language church at the invitation of Strasbourg's great reformer, Martin Bucer, who also introduced him to the widow who would later become Calvin's wife. The three years in Strasbourg was a productive time in Calvin's life: he managed to translate *Institutes* into French, prepare a second edition of the Latin version, and write a major commentary on Romans. In 1541, however, his exile came to an end. Calvin was invited back to Geneva to resume his program of religious reform.

From 1541 until his death in 1564, Calvin was able to pursue his program of theological reflection and application. Although Calvin is remembered primarily as a theologian and biblical commentator, his experience of the realities of public life in the cosmopolitan imperial city of Strasbourg had given him a new confidence to address the issue of Christianity in the public arena. Calvin's second Geneva period was marked by episodes of controversy (the burning of the Protestant heretic Michael Servetus was only the most notorious), disagreement with the city council, and personal unpopularity. It was also, however, a time in which Calvin's influence expanded considerably, particularly in his native France. By his death, there was a growing and powerful Calvinist presence in France, which can be seen as triggering the wars of religion in that country.

Calvin understood Christianity as a faith that engages the realities of both personal and public life. He had considerable interest in the development of an authentic Christian theology, and was well aware of the importance of issues of personal piety and spirituality. Yet his vision of the Christian faith extended far beyond the piety of a privatized faith or the cerebral conundrums of an intellectualized theology. Theology for Calvin offered a framework for engaging with public life.

A culture of free enterprise flourished in Geneva, in large part thanks to Calvin's benign attitude towards economics and finance. A comparison with Luther is instructive here. Luther's economic outlook — like his social thought in general — was heavily conditioned by the social realities of the unsophisticated rural German territories he set out to reform. His was a world preoccupied with the problems of late feudal rural life, especially the tensions between peasantry and nobility. Although Luther was clearly aware of some of the economic issues of his day — such as whether money should be loaned at interest — he did not understand the issues dominating urban finance. Luther had no conception of the economic forces that were beginning to transform Germany from a feudal nation of peasant agriculturalists into a society with an emergent capitalist economy. In his treatise "On Trade and Usury," written in the summer of 1524, Luther adopted a strongly critical attitude towards those engaged in any form of commercial activity. The fact that Luther's economic thought was hostile to any form of capitalism largely reflects his unfamiliarity with the sophisticated world of finance then emerging in the public life of the cities.

Calvin, however, was perfectly aware of the financial realities at Geneva and their implications. Although he did not develop an "economic theory" in any comprehensive sense of the term, he appears to have been fully cognizant of basic economic principles, recognizing the productive nature of both capital and human work. He praised the division of labor for its economic benefits and the way it emphasizes human interdependence and social existence. The right of individuals to possess property, denied by the radical wing of the Reformation, Calvin upheld. He recognized that passages in the Book of Deuteronomy relating to business ethics belonged to a bygone age; he refused to let the rules of a primitive Jewish agrarian society have binding force upon the progressive, modern, and urban Geneva of his time. Calvin dealt with the absolute prohibition upon lending money at interest (usury), for example, by arguing that it was merely an accommodation to the specific needs of a primitive society. Since there was no similarity between such a society and Geneva — interest is merely rent paid on capital, after all — he allowed lenders to charge a variable rate of interest. Calvin was sensitive to the pressures upon capital in a more or less free market, and believed that the ethical aims of the usury prohibition could be safeguarded by other means.

Calvin also articulated a work ethic that strongly encouraged the development of Geneva's enterprise culture. He taught that the individual believer has a vocation to serve God in the world — in every sphere of human existence — lending a new dignity and meaning to ordinary work. Calvin agreed that the world should be treated with contempt to the extent that it is not God, and is too easily mistaken for him; yet, it is the creation of God, to be affirmed at least to a degree. "Let believers get used to a contempt of the present life that gives rise to no hatred of it, or ingratitude towards God. . . . Something that is neither blessed nor desirable in itself can become something good for the devout." Christians are thus to inhabit the world with joy and gratitude, without becoming trapped within it. A degree of critical detachment must accompany Christian affirmation of the world as God's creation and gift. Christians are to live in the world, while avoiding falling into that world, becoming immersed within and swallowed by it.

To appreciate the significance of Calvin's work ethic, it is necessary to understand the intense distaste with which the early Christian tradition, illustrated by the monastic writers, regarded work. For Eusebius of Caesarea, the perfect Christian life was one devoted to serving God, untainted by physical labor. Those who chose to work for a living were second-rate Christians. The early monastic tradition appears to have inherited this attitude, with the result that work often came to be seen as a debasing and demeaning activity, best left to one's social — and spiritual — inferiors. If the social patricians of ancient Rome regarded work as below their status, it has to be said that a spiritual aristocracy appears to have developed within early Christianity with equally negative and dismissive attitudes towards manual labor. Such attitudes probably reached their height during the Middle Ages.

Scholars are much divided about the spiritual status of work in the Middle Ages. The Benedictine model of monasticism, with its stress on *ora et labora,* undoubtedly attributed great dignity to manual labor, though the first duty of the monk was always the Divine Office, called his "Opus Dei." It has been urged by some that the Benedictines, with their vast network of monastic enterprises, were in fact "the first capitalists." However that may be, there also persisted a widespread perception in medieval Christianity that those who worked "in the world," as distinct from monastics and clerics more generally, were engaged in a less worthy way of life and, indeed, were second-class Christians. Certainly that perception, combined with various corruptions of monasticism so caustically criticized by Erasmus and others, led Reformers such as Luther and Calvin to sharply contrast the monastic call "from the world" with the authentically Christian call "into the world."

In this view, Christians were called to be priests to the world, purifying and sanctifying its everyday life from within. Luther stated this point succinctly when commenting on Genesis 13:13: "What seem to be secular works are actually the praise of God and represent an obedience which is well-pleasing to him." There were no limits to this notion of calling. Luther even extolled the religious value of housework, declaring that although "it has no obvious appearance of holiness, yet these very household chores are more to be valued than all the works of monks and nuns."

Underlying this new attitude is the notion of the vocation or "calling." God calls his people, not just to faith, but to express that faith in quite definite areas of life. Whereas monastic spirituality regarded vocation as a calling out of the world into the desert or the monastery, Luther and Calvin regarded vocation as a calling into the everyday world. The idea of a calling or vocation is first and foremost about being called by God, to serve him within his world. Work was thus seen as an activity by which Christians could deepen their faith, leading it on to new qualities of commitment to God. Activity within the world, motivated, informed, and sanctioned by Christian faith, was the supreme means by which the believer could demonstrate his or her commitment and thankfulness to God. To do anything for God, and to do it well, was the fundamental hallmark of authentic Christian faith. Diligence and dedication in one's everyday life are, Calvin thought, a proper response to God.

For Calvin, God places individuals where he wants them to be, which explains Calvin's criticism of human ambition as an unwillingness to accept the sphere of action God has allocated to us. Social status is an irrelevance, a human invention of no spiritual importance; one cannot allow the human evaluation of an occupation's importance to be placed above the judgment of God who put you there. All human work is capable of "appearing truly respectable and being considered highly important in the sight of God." No occupation, no calling, is too mean or lowly to be graced by the presence of God.

The work of believers is thus seen to possess a significance that goes far beyond the visible results of that work. It is the person working, as much as the resulting work, that is significant to God. There is no distinction between spiritual and temporal, sacred and secular work. All human work, however lowly, is capable of glorifying God. Work is, quite simply, an act of praise — a potentially productive act of praise. Work glorifies God, it serves the common good, and it is something through which human creativity can express itself. The last two, it must be stressed, are embraced by the first. As Calvin's English follower William Perkins put it, "The true end of our lives is to do service to God in serving of man."

This insight is important in assessing certain aspects of the Reformation work ethic. Calvin, for example, weighs in strongly in support of St. Paul's injunction, "If someone does not work, then he should not eat" (2 Thessalonians 3:10). Several modern writers have severely criticized Calvin for that view, arguing that his comments demonstrate his insensitivity to the needs of the unemployed. Calvin's primary target, however, appears to have been quite different: the French aristocrats who sought refuge in Geneva and felt that their social status placed them above the need to work. They would not work; for Calvin, the common human obligation is to labor in the garden of the Lord, in whatever manner is commensurate with one's God-given gifts and abilities on the one hand, and the needs of the situation on the other. The common obligation to work is the great social leveler, a reminder that all human beings are created equal by God.

In many ways, Calvin's work ethic can be seen as a development of Paul's injunction to the Corinthian Christians: "Each one should retain the place in life that the Lord assigned to him and to which God has called him" (1 Corinthians 7:17). Calvin emphasized that the everyday activity of ordinary Christians has deep religious significance. The English poet George Herbert expressed this insight eloquently:

Teach me, my God and King,
In all things thee to see;
And what I do in anything
To do it as for thee.

A servant with this clause
Makes drudgery divine;
Who sweeps a room, as for thy laws,
Makes that and the action fine.

So who can learn from Calvin today? It is ironic that those who perhaps are most willing to listen to Calvin are also those who have most to learn from him. American evangelicalism is a complex phenomenon, and I have no wish to misrepresent it through simplification. However, it is fair to say that most evangelicals — and I write as one who gladly and positively identifies with this movement — regard the sixteenth-century Reformation as a period of heroic renewal of the Christian faith and triumphant rediscovery of the meaning of Scripture.

Yet many American evangelicals are ambivalent about engaging — as Calvin urged — with social and political matters. To become involved in such affairs is, they fear, to compromise the integrity of one's faith, to risk contamination by the sin of the world. Faith is a private matter, and is best kept that way. In making these observations, I must stress that I am not dismissing them; they represent serious concerns that reflect a perceptive appreciation of what can all too easily happen through uncritical immersion in the affairs of the world.

Calvin encourages believers to get involved — to be salt in the world. For Calvin, it is entirely possible to maintain integrity of faith while injecting a Christian presence and influence within society. This vision of a Christian society held a powerful appeal to our forebears: John Winthrop (1588-1649), the first Puritan governor of Massachusetts, even sought to build on the basis of the gospel a Christian civilization in the New World. Perhaps that vision lies beyond our reach — but it remains a challenge and stimulus to our thinking.

We can see the importance of this vision in Carl Henry's critique of fundamentalism in the late 1940s. Henry argued that fundamentalists did not present Christianity as a worldview, with a distinctive social vision, but chose to concentrate on personal conversion, only one aspect of the Christian proclamation. As a result, they presented an impoverished and reduced gospel to the world, radically defective in its social vision. Fundamentalism was too other worldly and anti-intellectual to gain a hearing amongst the educated public, and was unwilling to concern itself with exploring how Christianity related to culture and social life in general. The seventy-five pages of Henry's *Uneasy Conscience of Modern Fundamentalism* (1947) — what Dirk Jellema labeled the "manifesto of neo-evangelicalism" — sounded a clarion call for cultural engagement on the part of evangelicals. Fundamentalism had totally failed to turn back the rising forces of modernism, achieving no significant impact upon the world of its day, because it failed to address the social problems of its time. Henry's argument was unquestionably of major importance in encouraging a new generation of evangelicals to engage society, rather than withdraw into isolated, defensive, and inward-looking enclaves.

Calvin reminds his modern-day successors that while such engagement runs many risks, it is essential nonetheless if Christians are to be the leaven where leavening is most needed. It is not merely evangelicals who need to hear this counsel. If Christianity is to remain a positive force and influence in American public life, all Christians need to be present within that life, as salt and light. To remain safely behind the barricades may seem more secure, and a lot less risky — but it denies us any chance of reforming, renewing, and recalling our culture. The legacy of John Calvin invites us to engage our world, and instructs us in how to do so with integrity.

Pascal: The First Modern Christian

EDWARD T. OAKES

A s a way of dividing up history into discrete, manageable wholes, the
habit of clustering events according to centuries is probably no more (or
less) superficial than any other. And surely it must be safer and more reliable
than bandying about such descriptive monikers as "the Age of Faith," "the
Enlightenment," "the Atomic Age," and so on, for at least the century-unit is
known to be arbitrary, stemming as it does from the decimal system of num-
bering, which itself probably arose from the happenstance of ten fingers on
the pair of human hands.

Unfortunately, the broad-stroke descriptive label, like some post-it note
that sticks to everything it touches, will often enough get applied to the
century marker in any case — despite the objections of more fastidious
historians, who rightly fear that this habit of nomenclature may seduce the
unwary. For such catch-all tags as "Age of Anxiety," "Age of Chivalry," etc.
can be wildly inaccurate, or at least too sweeping. And no name for a century has been more misleading than that often used for the seventeenth:
the Age of Reason. Not only did this century see the worst of the witch-
hunting craze, but it also had to endure the Thirty Years War (1618-1648),
at root a European civil war of religion — and, like all wars of religion, a
clash of unbridled irrationality.

Yet just as centuries take on a certain inevitable identity from the very
habit of invoking them so often (hence this Millennium Series), so too do
these centuries soon come to assume the very descriptive characteristics by
which they have so frequently been identified. Not for nothing has the seventeenth century, despite its infamous displays of irrationality, been

76

known as the Age of Reason. Any century that began with René Descartes (1596-1650) as a five-year-old boy and concluded with Voltaire (1694-1778) as a seven-year-old, and during which Isaac Newton (1642-1727) and Gottfried Leibniz (1646-1716) lived most of their lives and Baruch Spinoza all of his (1632-1677), is bound to strike later centuries as an eminently rational era.

However repellent and violent the wars of religion were or however vehement the waning years of the witch-burning craze undoubtedly must have been, we cannot help but see the seventeenth century in terms of what our civilization has embraced and what, on the basis of that embrace, it has abjured. Wars of religion and witch-burning appall. Reason is hailed as the splendor of our species (yes, even today, despite what the Nietzscheans and Heideggerians might claim). Thus the Age of Reason is celebrated for what we most value in it, and in ourselves. We condemn its horrors, but only on the basis of its glories.

Indeed, very few textbooks in the history of philosophy would deny to Descartes, that quintessential man of the seventeenth century, the title of Founding Father of modern philosophy — and precisely because of his systematic and methodical elevation of reason. His method for rational inquiry, based on consistently held doubt toward all doctrinaire assumptions of the human mind, is usually seen as modernity's decisive breakout from the fettering chains of the medieval synthesis, which itself was formed from a prior fusion of reason and faith painstakingly soldered together over several centuries in the late Middle Ages. Because of Descartes, reason now regards itself as a fully adult faculty, free at last of the tutelage of dogma and tradition. It is to Descartes, above all, that we owe the idea of rationality as an all-purpose acid through which every tenaciously held belief of the human mind must pass.

In that setting Blaise Pascal (1623-1662) emerges as the man who became, as I shall argue in the rest of this essay, "the first modern Christian." I would even include in that judgment the deep reticence and privacy of his spiritual life, for Pascal rarely revealed the movements of his soul to any but his most trusted spiritual directors. Modernity often regards religion as a private affair of the heart and looks askance at too public displays of religious emotion; and there too Pascal strikes a remarkably modern note. Except for a few passing references in his letters, he rarely mentioned even the most important biographical milestones that determined his career. In fact, it is only because he sewed a parchment memorial of the event inside his coat pocket that history knows of the most important incident in his life — his "Night of Fire" on November 23, 1654, when for about two hours he was overwhelmed by tears of joy at the realization that the God of the philosophers was not the God of the Bible. No doubt he had always recognized what history has since come to acknowledge: that his legacy to us is due more to his thought than to his life.

He was born in the city of Clermont-Ferrard, in the south-central region of Auvergne, in 1623. His father was a government official, mostly in the royal court system, who at death (in 1651) left a comfortable sum to his one son and two daughters. In 1631 the father moved to Paris and later took up a post as tax assessor in Rouen, a tedious job that required long hours of dreary number-crunching. Seeing these grinding labors of his father, son Blaise struck upon the idea of building him a computer, the first ever invented and which is still on display in Paris at the *Conservatoire des Arts et Métiers*.

This remarkable achievement had already been foreshadowed by an event recounted by his older sister Gilberte. Blaise's father had assumed the entire responsibility for his son's education and had forbidden the boy to study or read geometry until he had first mastered Latin and Greek. But one day the father happened to come upon his precocious twelve-year-old, with charcoal and scrap paper on the floor, working out, totally untutored, Euclid's geometry up to the thirty-second proposition. Whether strictly true or merely *bien trouvé*, the story points to Pascal's universally acknowledged mathematical genius. In 1639, for example, at the age of sixteen, he wrote an essay on conic sections; and toward the end of his life he laid the foundations of the infinitesimal calculus, integral calculus, and the calculus of probabilities in a work that inspired Newton and Leibniz, more or less simultaneously and more or less independently of each other, to bring the development of calculus to where it is today. (Newton and Leibniz later got into a nasty dispute about who first discovered calculus, time that would have been better spent acknowledging their mutual debt to Pascal.)

The accidents of Pascal's biography also illuminate, at least partly, his famous attack on those sworn enemies of Jansenist theology, the Jesuit moralists, who were not loath to point out how Jansenism bore certain affinities with French Huguenot Calvinism. Now the great center of Jansenist theology and spirituality at that time was the convent of Port-Royal, where Pascal's younger sister Jacqueline had entered and which the Jesuits eventually prevailed upon an aging King Louis XIV to close once

Popes Innocent X, Alexander VII, and Clement XI had successively declared Jansenism a heresy. Although the convent only closed after Pascal's death, persecution of anyone associated with Port-Royal had already begun in his lifetime. Needless to say, the primary victims of this highhanded example of ecclesiastical *Machtpolitik* were not the Jansenist theologians (all male) but a convent of pious women who cared little for the subtleties of tractates on grace but who knew their Jansenist spiritual directors to be holy men. Such considerations meant nothing to an absolutist king and his Jesuit confessors, however, and royal persecution of the convent remained relentless, a campaign that made Pascal an enemy of the Jesuits for the rest of his life.

An essay treating Pascal's wider millennial significance cannot discuss in any detail the nature of his rather arcane dispute with the moral theologians of the Society of Jesus. But of his *Provincial Letters,* the collection of polemical tracts that had been provoked by the dispute, the last word should perhaps be given to the balanced judgment of T. S. Eliot: "He undoubtedly abused the art of quotation, as a polemical writer can hardly help but do; but there were abuses for him to abuse." Eliot is not excusing Pascal's ferocity here, even in the act of admitting that his targets deserved criticism. Quite the contrary, Eliot gets exactly the right balance when he says that "as polemic [these letters] are surpassed by none, not by Demosthenes, or Cicero, or Swift. [But] they have the limitation of all polemic and forensic: they persuade, they seduce, they are unfair."

Of course if this were all there was to Pascal, he would be merely the curiosity of the specialist, the fit subject of research for the historian of mathematics or the scholar of Counter-Reformation theology in France. But Pascal is more, much more. What makes him so utterly remarkable, indeed so remarkably *modern,* is the fact that he became the first Christian apologist both to absorb the Cartesian apotheosis of reason and to fight against its acidic effects, often using Descartes's own principles. In fact, so thoroughly did Pascal absorb the Cartesian outlook that from time to time one will find a philosophy textbook that classifies Pascal as the first and most influential member of the Cartesian school — a categorization which would certainly have come as a surprise to Pascal himself, most of whose references to Descartes in the jottings that make up the *Pensées* are derogatory. (Two examples: "Descartes useless and uncertain." "Write against those who probe science too deeply. Descartes.")

But perhaps there is a certain justice in this unhelpful pigeonholing of

Pascal as a Cartesian, especially when one considers his essay "The Spirit of Geometry and the Art of Persuasion." Here more than elsewhere he strikes the Cartesian note, as when he suggests that "logic has perhaps borrowed the rules of geometry without understanding their force." As with Descartes, and Spinoza after him, the ideal rational method for Pascal is what he calls the "geometrical" method, using mathematical rules of inference from accepted or self-evident axioms. Pascal means to set his purely mathematical form of inference over against the logical method of Aristotle, especially as it had been developed and extended by the medieval schoolmen. In this he is clearly presuming, as did Descartes, that medieval logic and "geometry" (in his sense) somehow conflict, to the detriment of all prior logic.

The two Frenchmen also share a noticeable dualism about the constitution of the human person, and here perhaps most of all we discover how much Descartes and Pascal have in common. Both men see human beings as a riddling composition of juxtaposed, antithetical essences (body and mind, flesh and spirit, extension and thinking), a dualism which in Pascal comes through most particularly in his famous definition of man as a "thinking reed." Both Descartes and Pascal, as true early moderns standing on the threshold of imminent discoveries of the universe's immensity from ever-improving telescopes, suspect the vast extension of space; but as true dualists (dualists who, moreover, give precedence to the mind) they also know that mind or consciousness can somehow possess and encompass that space in the very act of knowing it.

Pascal differs from Descartes's rather bloodless rationalism, however, in the explicitly theological implications he will try to draw from this anthropological dualism. He is alert, as Descartes rarely is, to the religious and ethical implications of this dualism of mind and body:

> *Thinking reed.* It is not in space that I must look for my dignity, but in the organization of my thoughts. *I shall have no advantage in owning estates.* Through space the universe grasps and engulfs me like a pinpoint; but through thought I can grasp it. . . . All our dignity consists, therefore, of thought. It is from there that we must be lifted up and not from space and time, which we could never fill. So let us work on thinking well. That is the principle of morality.

No doubt this passage will strike most readers as a remarkable summary of Cartesian metaphysics, especially in its reliance on the famous distinction between the nonspatial "thinking thing" (mind) and the space-occupying "extended thing" (body). But even here we can pick up the characteristic tone of the Pascalian stress on morality: far from trying à la Descartes to take this initial dualism as the basis on which to build a rickety philosophical superstructure, Pascal wants to see in the baffling juxtaposition of these two irreconcilable substances the very pathos of human existence itself. "Man's nature is entirely natural, *wholly animal,*" he concedes. "There is nothing that cannot be made natural." But that is also why, he says, "there is nothing that cannot be lost."

Nothing, then, is exempt from the death sentence of nature, not even knowledge, not even spirit — which is why, as Pascal says, "man's true nature, his true good and true virtue, and true religion cannot be known separately." In other words, to admit the essential animality of human nature, *right through to the soul,* becomes for Pascal the beginning of rational wisdom. Indeed, morality begins with this admission: not in a flight from nature but in a recognition of its misery and corruption. (Note that Pascal's first conclusion from his mind/body dualism is not epistemological, but moral: there is no point in owning vast "spatial" estates, he says above, precisely because the soul is nonspatial.)

In fact few thinkers, when read carefully, would seem less Cartesian than Pascal, even in his philosophy of science, which at first glance seems so Cartesian, with its praise of the "geometrical" mind. Actually, for all his brilliance as a mathematician and despite his awe before the geometrical method, Pascal gives a much more ringing defense of the empirical method than any of the British empiricists managed to do, and he certainly grants to the senses a much larger role than any of his fellow Continental Rationalists could muster. Today we can see that the British Empiricists went too far and misinterpreted rationality as a mere generalization of sensation, while the Continental Rationalists went to the other extreme because they could not grant the exalted title "knowledge" to any but rational truths. But Pascal, anticipating the errors of both schools and sounding almost like a disciple of W. V. Quine *avant la lettre,* was able to balance rational and empirical, *a priori* and *a posteriori* reasoning with a remarkably contemporary note. "When we say that the diamond is the hardest of all bodies," he observes in his fragmentary *Treatise on the Vacuum,* "we mean of all bodies with which we are acquainted. We cannot and ought not to include those bodies of which we are entirely ignorant. . . . For in all matters in which proof consists in experiences and not in demonstrations, one cannot make any universal assertion save by general enumeration of all the parts and of all the different cases."

This principle might seem obvious today, but its application had an unsettling effect on the mind of contemporary natural philosophers trained in medieval scholastic physics. In 1648 Pascal's brother-in-law carried a barometer up a mountain and observed how the level of mercury changed with the height of the mountain. Pascal then repeated the experiment by checking the mercury levels at various heights inside a Parisian church tower, the results of which prompted him to exclaim: "Nature has no abhorrence of a vacuum, she makes no effort to avoid it. . . . Due to their lack of knowledge of this phenomenon, people have invented a wholly imaginary horror of a vacuum." As noted philosopher of science Richard H. Popkin rightly observes: "Combining his ingeniously derived experimental data with a clear analysis of the possible explanatory hypotheses, Pascal arrived at one of the major achievements of seventeenth-century science."

But Pascal is even more noticeably anti-Cartesian in his concern for the Christian religion. Descartes famously loathed theological disputes and avoided their entanglements whenever possible. Pascal, as his acrimonious debates with the Jesuits attest, entered the fray of theological infighting with startling gusto and vehemence. But what most of his contemporaries, both friend and foe, failed during his lifetime to see about his motivation emerged only after his death, when his younger sister gathered together the shards and *disjecta membra* of his notes for a projected work of apologetics and published them in the form we know today as the *Pensées*.

From this remarkable work we now realize that Pascal saw himself, above all, as Christ's apologete and defender against Christianity's rationalist scoffers (whereas Descartes in contrast knew himself primarily, indeed only, as a scientist and philosopher). No doubt Pascal always remained heavily indebted to Descartes's dualism of mind and matter, but in his apologetics for Christianity he transforms Cartesian dualism into merely one aspect of a much deeper and more central dualism: not between spirit and matter but between God's holiness and human misery, not between soul and body but between God's infinity and man's sin. Christ came to heal these more agonizing divisions — divisions rooted not in incompatible metaphysical essences but in the pathos of the enfleshed soul trapped in sin. The Incarnation thus becomes a balm applied to man's riven soul, torn not so much between spirit and flesh as between despair and pride.

[The Christian religion] teaches men both these truths: that there is a God of whom we are capable, and that a corruption in our nature makes us unworthy of Him. It is equally important for us to know both these points; for it is equally dangerous for man to know God without knowing his own wretchedness, and to know his wretchedness without knowing the Redeemer who can cure him of it. Knowledge of only one of these points leads either to the arrogance of the philosophers, who have known God and not their own wretchedness, or to the despair of the atheists, who know their wretchedness without knowing the Redeemer.

We can see from these remarks that for Pascal Descartes's dualism is missing a crucial element: he has failed to provide an analysis of the *moral* dangers to which the human spirit is prone precisely because of its capacity for an infinite reach to the very ends of the universe. Pascal openly affirms with Descartes that our capacity to know the universe makes us masters, in some paradoxical sense, of the universe we conceive. But our capacity to "grasp" the universe and transform it into a mental construct of our knowing powers remains both paradox and pathos: we always accomplish these acts of knowing as puny, pathetic, and vulnerable bodies, whose corruption eventually leads to death.

This knowing mind, however, would rather remain enamored of its cognitive powers than acknowledge that this knowing power is an organic function of the brain. (Philosopher John Searle calls the brain "cognitive meat," which nicely captures in the minor key of neuroscience Pascal's more metaphysical definition in the major key of man as a "thinking reed.") Fearing the inevitable dissolution of its powers, the mind hides from itself the reality of its own insignificance. Second only to cognition itself, the most notable fact of the human mind lies in its tendency to forget the realities of its corruption and death.

Hence the central temptation of man is always pride. (Thus did the Serpent tempt Adam and Eve.) For Pascal, pride is a deeply functional sin: it works to help us forget. The mind shrinks from recognizing its status as a thinking reed by hiding under a carapace of pride. Characteristically, Descartes failed to notice this pathos; a missing element that, like the non-barking dog that became the decisive clue in the Sherlock Holmes story, tells us why Cartesian philosophy is more culprit than detective, more likely, that is, to lead us astray than to bring us to the truth.

But despite a few stray remarks in the *Pensées* that attack Descartes, Pascal's intent there is not, fundamentally, polemical. Throughout this fascinating book of almost random observations the reader soon picks up the author's driving motivation. Pascal above all wants to explain to his post-Cartesian contemporaries how the pathos of human nature has its own "balm in Gilead," a healing ointment in Jesus Christ, who is the very divine incarnation of these human oppositions. But of course Jesus Christ can only be accepted *as* Christ (the "anointed one") if one first admits that human nature needs his healing balm. Christ's coming on earth thus has the odd effect of eliciting hate precisely because his presence in history will reopen wounds that our distracted culture thought had been healed not by his balm but by the iodine of hyperactivity.

No wonder, then, that modernity since the Enlightenment has taken scandal in Jesus Christ. Even inside our own culture, which is often called "post"-modern because of its self-image of being more accommodating to local traditions and intercultural understanding than was Enlightened modernity, Christianity still is made to feel something like the bastard son who shows up uninvited at the annual family picnic. Inside all the talk about multiculturalism, contemporary culture often balks at including Christianity in its "gorgeous mosaic." This uneasiness has sometimes been dubbed the "ABC Rule," meaning "anything but Christianity." Undoubtedly Pascal would amend that to mean "anyone but Christ," for at root that is where the scandal lies. Christianity's scandal is not just itself (though it is that as well, which is no doubt why the Pope wants the Church formally to repent of her institutional sins); its *real* scandal is Jesus Christ. And *he* is the stumbling block precisely because to accept him is first of all to admit one's hopelessness without him. Pride and life in Christ are inherently incompatible.

> Pride tells us we can know God without Jesus Christ, in effect that we can communicate with God without a mediator. But this only means that we are communicating with a God who is the [prideful] result that comes from being known without a mediator. Whereas those who have known God through a mediator know their own wretchedness. Not only is it impossible to know God without Jesus Christ, it is also useless. . . . [For] knowing God without knowing our wretchedness leads to pride. Knowing our wretchedness without knowing God leads to despair. Knowing Jesus Christ is the middle course, because in Him we find both God and our wretchedness.

Because he wants the Incarnation to be a cure appropriate to the disease and because the death of Christ on the cross is indeed a most radical cure, implying a serious illness, Pascal is usually categorized as a "pessimistic" thinker — he wants his readers to see how far advanced the disease infecting them really is. And certainly he can be unsparing in his portrayal of the fleshly corruption and frail constitution of that "bruised and crushed reed" that is the human body. No doubt he could describe the corruption of the flesh so well partly because his own health was so appallingly bad, perhaps the worst of any Christian mystic with the exception of Teresa of Ávila and Adrienne von Speyr. (In fact, at his autopsy it was discovered that the fontanel — the "soft spot" on an infant's skull — had never been closed over in Pascal's case by the formation of skull bone, so that Pascal lived his entire life with an unclosed cranium, which certainly provides a weird intensity to his definition of man as a "thinking reed.") But in depicting human wretchedness Pascal never wallows in scenes of grim despair but simply faces the human condition as it is, universally. In fact for Pascal, as for Dostoevsky later, the real issue comes down not to the sheer immensity of human suffering but more crucially to the fact that human suffering only has to occur *once* for the issue of man's predicament to be raised.

But Dostoevsky (or at least his fictional character Ivan Karamazov) takes the fact of just one child suffering and on that basis assumes the role of being humanity's "prosecuting attorney," as it were, charging God to justify himself as God in the face of that one moment of evil. Pascal lived well before this style of what is often called "protest atheism," but if he were transported to Ivan Karamazov's celestial courtroom as "attorney for the defense," as it were, he would surely turn the argument around and put the challenge to the whole courtroom: anyone who would presume to act as *spectator* to this suffering (as judge and jury must do in order to fulfill their roles) has a challenge to face too. What Pascal would say, in other words, is that as long as we take the spectator's part and view human suffering from the outside, then, no matter how happy our circumstances are at the moment, we must know ourselves fundamentally as wretched beings. "Imagine a number of men in chains, all under sentence of death," he would say to the courtroom as he did in the *Pensées*, "some of whom are each day butchered in the sight of the others; those remaining see their own condition in that of their fellows, and looking at each other with grief and despair await their turn. This is an image of the human condition."

Especially in this era of terrorists parading their hostages in front of the world's television screens, or hijackers holding a pistol to the head of an airline pilot for all the world to behold, or high school students hiding under cafeteria tables while their friends are being murdered by their own peers, we immediately recognize the truth of what Pascal is saying. But Pascal does not intend to force his readers to wallow in this misery. Rather, his depiction of the human condition is meant only to create the first opening through which we hear God's response to that misery. Such a response, like the answer of the Almighty to Job, will be no courtroom defense speech. Jansenist that he was, Pascal firmly believed that "God owes us nothing," and so Dostoevsky's formulation would have been inconceivable to him. And yet, however inadequate it might be in the eyes of the "protest atheist" (who, as a spectator of suffering, must perforce judge God from the outside), God's answer is not nothing. But that answer cannot even be heard if we do not admit the realities of the human condition in all their bleakness. Even as spectators, we suffer what we are forced to see. Television screens force us to become spectators of appalling suffering, but the situation they reveal is rooted in everyone's nature. There is no escape from its pathos, only balm for our wounds — if we are willing to accept the astringency of the ointment.

Of course, not many want that kind of painful healing, making it well-nigh inevitable that we will avail ourselves of distractions from our woes. Few words, in fact, are more crucial to Pascal than *divertissement,* usually translated as "diversion" or "distraction." One of Pascal's most famous observations, found in nearly every anthology of quotations, holds that "all the misfortunes of men derive from one single thing, their inability to remain at repose in a room." Far from being merely the obiter dictum of a dry cynic, Pascal's remark actually forms the opening gambit of his Christian apologetics, for he knows that "being unable to cure death, wretchedness, and ignorance," and being not too fond of the medicine of Christ on offer either, "men have decided, in order to be happy, not to think about such things." "Pessimist" that he is, however, Pascal refuses to let us evade God's answer to our plight just because we would rather not advert to our distress in the first place. "That is why men are so fond of hustle and bustle," he says. "That is why prison is such a fearful punishment; that is why the pleasures of solitude are so incomprehensible."

This craving for distraction is so overriding and exigent that for Pascal it actually constitutes the driving force of ambition. In one sharply worded paragraph in the *Pensées,* he asserts that the main joy of being a king is the opportunity it affords for endless distraction, since courtiers are continually trying to keep the king's mind off his mortality and provide him every kind of pleasure. "A king is surrounded by people whose only thought is to divert him so that he might be kept from thinking about himself, because, king though he is, he becomes unhappy as soon as he thinks about himself."

But what applies to the ambitions of a king applies equally well to the motivations of all men. We crave distractions because we do not want to face the realities of the human condition. And because we are unwilling to admit our despair, we perforce cannot face the thought of applying the appropriate balm to heal these unacknowledged wounds. Consequently we hurl ourselves into an endless round of diversions, jobs, hobbies, etc., all to avoid our nature as thinking reeds:

> Man is obviously made for thinking. Therein lies all his dignity and his merit; and his whole duty is to think as he ought. Now the order of thought is to begin with ourselves, and with our Author and our end. But what does the world think about? Never about that, but about dancing, playing the lute, singing, writing verse, jousting and fighting, becoming a king, without ever thinking what it means to be a king or to be a man.

Like Kierkegaard and Heidegger after him, Pascal was an acute student of boredom, and saw in this phenomenon (actually rather puzzling when one thinks about it) the clue to the very pathos of the human condition. Generally speaking, says Pascal, "we think either of present woes or of threatened miseries." But moments occur in almost everyone's experience when life reaches a temporary pause of homeostasis, when we feel quite safe on every side, when bad health does not threaten, when bill collectors are not baying at the door, when rush-hour traffic is light and the weather pleasant. But precisely at such moments "boredom on its own account emerges from the depths of our hearts, where it is naturally rooted, and poisons our whole mind." Not just the king craves diversion. So terrified are we of boredom that the king's ambition is our own.

I have called Pascal "the first modern Christian" because, among other reasons, our civilization, in contrast to all other past civilizations, gets its very identity from the sheer range of distractions that have now been made available to us, from hundreds of channels on cable TV to over a thousand video cassettes on the shelf of any self-respecting video rental agency to the millions of websites on the Internet, group activities of every sort imaginable, aerobics classes, talk-show radio on the air twenty-four hours a day, and so on. As the literary journalist Norman Cousins observed in his book *Human Options:*

> Our own age is not likely to be distinguished in history for the large numbers of people who insisted on finding the time to think. Plainly, this is not the Age of Meditative Man. . . . Substitutes for repose are a billion dollar business. Almost daily, new antidotes for contemplation spring into being and leap out from store counters. Silence, already the world's most critical shortage, is in danger of becoming a nasty word. Modern man may or may not be obsolete, but he is certainly wired for sound and he twitches as naturally as he breathes.

Of course no one denies the legitimate need for entertainment or the role that diversion plays in generating demand for the works of art that have become the glory of our species. Often life achieves its goal of testifying to its own goodness as worth living when a human being is able to enjoy the highest benefits of culture. I personally count myself most glad to be alive when I am enjoying a good meal with a friend, listening to Mozart in the privacy of my room, or reading a good book. Nor, despite his seeming Jansenist severity, would Pascal contemn such pleasures. Even he, the least therapeutic writer imaginable, admits that diversions can help to heal the beset soul ("that is why the man who lost his only son a few months ago and who was so troubled and oppressed this morning by lawsuits and quarrels is for the moment [because of a fleeting diversion] not thinking about it").

But our extraordinary obsession with entertainment and distraction constitutes perhaps *the* hallmark of our civilization in contrast to past cultures. From the time the clock radio goes off in the morning to the late-night talk shows, the average denizen of contemporary culture need never be alone, encounter silence, or have to listen to the voice within. As Pascal says: "We run heedlessly into the abyss after putting something in front of us to keep from seeing the precipice." Or as the French poet Paul Claudel says, speaking of the New Testament's Book of Revelation: "What if, beneath all this revelry and group cheer, there were something seething under our feet?"

To the journalistic mind, all this gloom-and-doom apologetic is going to sound like the grim Calvinist sermons in *The Scarlet Letter* that poured forth from the tormented pulpit of the aptly named Rev. Mr. Arthur Dimmesdale. Schooled by the plot of this *Urmyth* of American Protestantism, the same journalistic mind will inevitably ask: What could be more life-denying than this constant dwelling on the dire straits of the human condition? And since Pascal owes so much to Calvinist doctrines of grace, is he not really the Catholic equivalent of the Rev. Mr. Dimmesdale?

No. Rather, the self-satisfied glee of the professional scoffer — the kind of opinion-monger who takes satisfaction in the fall of Jimmy Swaggart, Jim and Tammy Bakker, or any other easy target — comes from a different motivation than a resentment against a supposedly life-denying Calvinist or Jansenist Christianity. Underneath the smug cluck-clucking at the fall of a Christian aiming for sanctity, Pascal will detect the "ABC rule" working its effect:

> *Order.* Men despise religion. They hate it and are afraid it may be true. The cure for this is first to show that religion is not contrary to reason, but worthy of reverence and respect. Next, make it attractive, make good men wish it were true, and then show that it is. Worthy of reverence because it really understands human nature. Attractive because it promises true good.

Of course, nothing could be further from Pascal's intention than to sweep all religions under the universal rubric of human religiosity and see them merely as aspects of one global "search for meaning." Enlightenment thinkers, who hoped to find a basis for international comity beyond the particularity of culture and religion, saw the modern pluriformity of religions as a problem. So too have postmodern thinkers, with their opposite privileging of the particular culture over against an allegedly "hegemonic" universal culture. Pascal, however, takes the multiplicity of religions to be a way of proving the truth of Christianity. Its very particularity, for Pascal, dramatically indicates its transcendental truth: "On the fact that the Christian religion is not unique: Far from being a reason for believing it not to be the true religion, it is on the contrary what proves it to be so."

Perhaps no sentence that came from Pascal's pen better encapsulates what makes him so modern as this apparent paradox. Nothing so beset, even fixated, the Enlightened mind of Pascal's time and in the century to follow than what has become known as the "scandal of particularity." If God's will to save is universal, how can it matter what one believes in particular? What difference does it make what religion one belongs to or believes in, since — as one is constantly hearing on the lips of nearly every American — "it's all the same God anyway"?

Second only to Dante, Pascal is Europe's most politically incorrect writer. He dares to raise the unmentionable topic of truth in religion, and even called one of the sections of his *Pensées* "Nature Is Corrupt: On the Falseness of Other Religions." In contrast to most reflection on the problem of world religions in today's academy, Pascal sees the "problem" as in fact essential for the truth of the Christian message:

> *That God wanted to be hidden.* If there were only one religion, God would be clearly manifest. If there were martyrs only in our religion, the same. God being therefore hidden, any religion which does not say that God is hidden is not true. And any religion which does not give us the reason why does not enlighten. Ours does all this. . . . If there were no obscurity man would not feel his corruption: if there were no light man could not hope for a cure. Thus it is not only right but useful that God should be partly concealed and partly revealed, since it is equally dangerous for man to know God without knowing his wretchedness as to know his own wretchedness without knowing God. "Truly God is hidden with you" (Isaiah 45:15).

But of course the key to finding this light is to search for it, and this once more brings us to the central difficulty: do we *want* the light of the truth? "Truth is so obscured nowadays and lies so well established that unless we love the truth we shall never recognize it."

So there are good reasons for Christianity to stress not only its uniqueness (every religion is unique in some way) but its inherent truth. Nothing is more awkward in our ecumenical age than for a religion to stress its possession of the truth. But Pascal would say to Christians that unless it is confident that it possesses the truth, Christianity will not have the confidence that it can apply the only salve that can heal the real wounds of humanity. As the former Marxist Leszek Kolakowski put it in his defense of Pascal:

> There are reasons why we need Christianity, but not just any kind of Christianity. We do not need a Christianity that makes political revo-

lution, that rushes to cooperate with so-called sexual liberation, that approves our concupiscence or praises our violence. There are enough forces in the world to do all these things without the aid of Christianity. We need a Christianity that will help us to move beyond the immediate pressures of life, that gives us insight into the basic limits of the human condition and the capacity to accept them, a Christianity that teaches us the simple truth that there is not only a tomorrow but a day after tomorrow as well, and that the difference between success and failure is rarely distinguishable.

But even this formulation puts the matter too weakly (one detects in Kolakowski's praise of Pascal the same weakness that has made him so diffident toward doctrinal Christianity throughout his published career). Far better perhaps is the judgment of T. S. Eliot, who to my mind has summed up Pascal's achievement best of all; and, as befits Pascal himself, he has done so in one sentence of unsurpassed accuracy and concision: "I can think of no Christian writer, not Newman even, more to be commended than Pascal to those who doubt, but who have the mind to conceive, and the sensibility to feel, the disorder, the futility, the meaninglessness, the mystery of life and suffering, and who can only find peace through a satisfaction of the whole being."

Pascal's was a remarkable achievement, made even more remarkable by one — often overlooked — detail: he died at the age of thirty-nine.

Rousseau and the Revolt Against Reason

MARY ANN GLENDON

I N 1749 THE ACADEMY OF DIJON offered a prize for the best essay on the question, "Has the restoration of the sciences and the arts contributed to the improvement of mores?" Most of the contestants must have vied in counting the ways "enlightenment" had raised the level of culture. By the middle of the eighteenth century, advances in science and technology had fueled faith in progress. It was widely believed that the human race was emerging from a long night of ignorance and superstition into an era when Reason at last would conquer age-old social and political problems. It was something of a sensation, therefore, when the palm went to a self-taught thirty-eight-year-old who answered the question with a resounding "No."

In the essay now known as his *First Discourse,* Jean-Jacques Rousseau argued that manners and morals had been corrupted as the arts and sciences had advanced. The arts had encouraged sensuality and license, while science had set up strange gods against true religion. Reason had been elevated over feeling, learning over plain goodness and honesty. City people looked down on country folk, and the rich more than ever lorded it over the poor. Political writers spoke less of virtue than of commerce. Society was overrun with scribblers who "smile contemptuously at such old names as patriotism and religion, and consecrate their talents and philosophy to the destruction and defamation of all that men hold sacred." Echoing pietistic warnings about vain learning, Rousseau asked: What is learning without virtue? What progress can there be without progress in goodness?

The *First Discourse* was followed by a cascade of writings in which Rousseau challenged the scientific rationalism of Voltaire and other well-known intellectuals who immodestly called themselves *les Lumières,* the enlightened ones. In the space of twelve years, the eccentric outsider produced a stream of works that made him the preeminent critic of modernity. Yet he was no traditionalist. Through his elevation of feeling over reason, he became the leading prophet of the ultramodern era that would succeed the so-called age of reason.

Rousseau was born in Calvinist Geneva in 1712, the son of a watchmaker and a mother who died from complications of childbirth. When the boy was ten, his father placed him in the care of an uncle who in turn sent him to live with a country pastor. These men provided him with a haphazard education, but the precocious youth never received any formal schooling. At fifteen, after an unhappy apprenticeship to an engraver, he struck out on his own for the nearby Duchy of Savoy. There, a parish priest commended the wandering lad to the hospitality of a woman of good works in Annecy.

Warmhearted Madame de Warens, the estranged wife of a landowner, was not your usual church lady. Though a convert to Catholicism and pious in her way, she did not believe in original sin, or Hell, or that it could be sinful to follow one's natural impulses. She took a fancy to the clever, awkward boy, and he developed an enduring attachment to her. Rousseau spent several formative years as a sort of cavalier-servant, and occasional sexual partner, to this woman, whom he called *Maman.* Under her protection, he read voraciously, gained a sense of his extraordinary mental powers, and learned enough about music to support himself as a copyist and teacher.

In 1744, after holding various menial positions — footman, tutor, secretary — in well-to-do households here and there, Rousseau settled in Paris, determined to be independent. There he became friendly with Diderot, and began his lifelong liaison with Thérèse Le Vasseur, a laundry maid in his residential hotel. According to the well-known story in Rousseau's *Confessions,* each of the five children born of this union was abandoned to a foundling home shortly after birth. The writer whose works had extolled the child-centered family explained to posterity that he had insisted on this "solution," over Thérèse's tearful protests, because he was too poor to provide for children, and that, besides, they would have interfered with his study and work.

(Rousseau's biographers, though skeptical of much of his autobiographical material, have always taken that tale at face value. There is reason to suppose, however, that the long-suffering Thérèse may not have complied with her consort's wishes. She and her ever-present mother treated their brilliant patron, in many respects, like a child or ward. They did not hesitate, for instance, to make financial arrangements with Rousseau's friends behind his back. It would have been quite in character for them, faced with his refusal to accept parental responsibility, to have placed the babies with members of their large, extended Catholic family.)

Rousseau's circumstances improved greatly after he won the Dijon prize. His cheeky, contrarian *First Discourse* brought him not only literary fame, but an entrée into polite society where, however, he would never be at ease. That essay was followed by his discourses on *Inequality* (the *Second Discourse*) and *Political Economy*, both destined to be landmarks in political philosophy. *Julie, ou la Nouvelle Héloïse,* which appeared in 1761, became the best-selling novel of the eighteenth century. *The Social Contract,* with ideas and phrases that would capture the imaginations of revolutionaries, and *Émile,* his enormously influential work on education, were both published in 1762.

That extraordinary burst of creativity was followed by a long period of physical and mental decline, the former mostly due to an agonizing disorder of the urinary tract, and the latter aggravated by persecution for the blasphemies that Catholics and Calvinists alike discerned in his work. Despite the sufferings, real and imagined, of his later years, Rousseau managed to produce the *Confessions, Dialogues,* and *Reveries of a Solitary Walker,* all published posthumously.

After his death in 1778, Rousseau's popularity soared to new heights. *Julie* and *Émile* continued to attract a wide readership, especially among women, while his political writings made him a cult hero to the leaders of the French Revolution. The century was one in which rulers and politicians were particularly open to the ideas of philosophers. Frederick II of Prussia, Catherine the Great, and Joseph II of Austria considered themselves enlightened monarchs and took pride in being advised by the likes of Voltaire. The American Founders were much influenced by the thinking of Locke and Montesquieu. When the French Revolution entered its radical phase, it was the ideas and catchphrases of Rousseau, more than any other thinker, that dominated the thinking and speaking of the insurgents.

Even today, Rousseau remains the preeminent expounder of challenging ideas about human beings, nature, politics, and history that must be reckoned with one way or another. Whether one finds him disturbing or stimulating, it is nearly impossible to remain unaffected by him. Like Plato and Nietzsche, he saw deeply into the most important questions and wrote about them so beautifully that, love him or hate him, we all stand in his shadow. As Allan Bloom once wrote, "His influence was overwhelming, and so well was it digested into the bloodstream of the West that it worked on everyone almost imperceptibly."

Rousseau's influence on political thought extended far beyond France and its Revolution. His early modern predecessors, Machiavelli, Hobbes, Locke, and Spinoza, had broken with the virtue-based political theories of the ancients and developed theories of government based on human nature as they thought it really was, rather than as it ought to be. Rousseau attacked this "new science of politics" at its foundations. He began his *Discourse on Inequality* by scoffing at previous attempts to account for the origins of government by describing what human beings must have been like in the "state of nature." The mythic tales told by Hobbes and Locke had recounted the progress of mankind from "a horrible state of war" (Hobbes) or from a "very precarious, very unsafe" existence (Locke) into a more secure way of life in organized society. According to Rousseau, such accounts had it backwards. Prior writers had failed to understand the natural condition of man, he claimed, because they "carried over to the state of nature ideas they had acquired in society; they spoke about savage man but they described civilized man." The complex fears and desires they attributed to our early ancestors could only have been produced by society.

Rousseau then presented his own version of pre-history as universal truth: "O man, of whatever country you are, and whatever your opinions may be, listen: behold your history as I have thought to read it, not in books written by your fellow creatures, who are liars, but in nature, which never lies." The earliest human, as Rousseau imagined him, was a simple, animal-like creature, "wholly wrapped up in the feeling of [his own] present existence." He was not inherently dangerous to his fellows as Hobbes had it. But neither was he fallen as the biblical tradition teaches. Rather, he must have led a "solitary," "indolent" life, satisfying his basic physical needs, mating casually without forming ties. He possessed a "natural feeling" of compassion for the suffering of other sentient beings that made him unwilling to harm others, unless (a big unless) his own self-preservation was at stake. He was not naturally endowed with reason, but existed in an unreflective state of pure being. The transition from this primitive state into civil society represented a "loss of real felicity," in Rousseau's view, rather than an unambiguous step forward.

Rousseau next took aim at the social contract theories of his predecessors. As he saw it, what drew human beings out of their primeval state was not rational calculation leading to agreement for the sake of self-preservation (as Hobbes and Locke thought), but rather a quality he called "perfectibility." Previous thinkers, he claimed, did not pay sufficient attention to the distinctively human capacity to change and develop, to transform oneself and to be transformed. In other words, they failed to consider the implications of the fact that human nature itself has a history. Or that human beings, through their capacity to form ideas, can to some extent shape that history. These were the insights of the *Discourse on Inequality* that won the admiration of such a dissimilar personality as Immanuel Kant and stirred the historical imaginations of Hegel and Marx.

With the development of human faculties, Rousseau continued, came language, family life, and eventually an era when families lived in simple tribal groups. That centuries-long stage of communal living, succeeding the state of nature and preceding organized society, he wrote, "must have been the happiest and most stable of epochs," which only a "fatal accident" could have brought to an end. That accident was precipitated by the ever-restless human mind that invented agriculture and metallurgy, which led in turn to the state of affairs where human beings lost their self-sufficiency and came to depend on one another for their survival. ("It is iron and wheat which have civilized men and ruined the human race.")

In contrast to Locke, who taught that property was an especially important, pre-political right, Rousseau wrote:

> The first man who, having enclosed a piece of ground, bethought himself of saying *This is mine,* and found people simple enough to believe him, was the real founder of civil society. From how many crimes, wars, and murders, from how many horrors and misfortunes might not any one have saved mankind by pulling up the stakes, or filling up the ditch, and crying to his fellows, "Beware of listening to this imposter, you are undone if you once forget that the fruits of the earth belong to us all, and the earth itself to nobody."

Contrary to Hobbes and Locke, Rousseau contended that it was civil society, not nature, that gave rise to a state of affairs that was always in danger of degenerating into war. Civil society begat governments and laws, inequality, resentment, and other woes. Governments and laws "bound new fetters on the poor, and gave new powers to the rich; which irretrievably destroyed natural liberty, eternally fixed the law of property and inequality, converted clever usurpation into unalterable right, and, for the advantage of a few ambitious individuals, subjected all mankind to perpetual labor, slavery, and wretchedness." It would be absurd to suppose, he went on, that mankind had somehow consented to this state of affairs where "the privileged few . . . gorge themselves with superfluities, while the starving multitude are in want of the bare necessities of life."

Though Rousseau's evocative imaginary depictions of primitive societies were to swell the tide of nineteenth-century romantic "nostalgia" for the simple life, he himself insisted that there was no escape from history. There was no going back, he explained, because human nature itself had changed: "The savage and the civilized man differ so much . . . that what constitutes the supreme happiness of one would reduce the other to despair." Natural man had been sufficient unto himself; man in civil society had become dependent on his fellows in countless ways, even to the point of living "in the opinions of others." Reprising the theme of his Dijon essay, Rousseau concluded that modern man, though surrounded by philosophy, civilization, and codes of morality, had little to show for himself but "honor without virtue, reason without wisdom, and pleasure without happiness."

The radical character of Rousseau's political thought is nowhere more apparent than in his treatments of reason and human nature. Together with early modern and Enlightenment thinkers, he rejected older ideas of a natural law discoverable through right reason. But by insisting that human beings are not naturally endowed with reason, he struck at the very core of the Enlightenment project, subordinating reason to feeling in a move that would characterize the politics of a later age. Like others within the modern horizon, he rejected the older view that human beings are naturally social or political. But by exalting individual solitude and self-sufficiency, he set himself apart from his fellow moderns, anticipating the hyper-individualism of a much later age — our own.

Not without justification, then, did Bloom call the *Discourse on Inequality* "the most radical work ever written, one that transformed the way people thought about the world." This one essay contained the germs of most of the themes Rousseau would develop in later works, and that would be further elaborated by others who came under his spell. Rousseau's lyrical descriptions of early man and simple societies fueled the nineteenth-century popular romantic revolt against classicism in art and literature. His criticism of property, together with his dark view of the downside of mutual dependence, made a deep impression on the young Karl Marx.

The thesis of the *Second Discourse,* that the most serious forms of injustice had their origins in civil society rather than in nature, foreshadowed Rousseau's famous charge at the beginning of *The Social Contract* that virtually all existing governments were illegitimate: "Man is born free; and everywhere he is in chains." Having raised the explosive issue of legitimacy, and sensing that Europe's old regimes were about to crumble, Rousseau turned to his most ambitious project to date: the question of how better governments might be established. "I want to see," he wrote, "if, in the civil order, there can be some legitimate and solid rule of administration, taking men as they are and the laws as they can be."

Like many critical theorists before and since, Rousseau was less successful at developing a positive political vision of his own than he had been at spotting flaws in the theories of others. In *The Social Contract,* he framed the problem of good government as that of finding a form of political association which would protect everyone's person and property, but within which each person would remain "as free as before." The solution he devised was an agreement by which everyone would give himself and all his goods to the community, forming a state whose legislation would be produced by the will of each person thinking in terms of all (the "general will"). The state's legitimacy would thus be derived from the people, who, in obeying the law, would be obeying themselves.

That solution to the problem of legitimate government would obviously require a special sort of citizen, a "new man" who could and would choose the general will over his own interests or the narrow interests of his group. The concept of the general will thus links *The Social Contract* to Rousseau's writings on nurture, education, and morals, particularly *Émile,* which contains his program for forming the sentiments of the young so that they will retain their natural goodness while living in civil society.

The legitimate state, as Rousseau imagined it, would need not only virtuous citizens, but an extraordinary "Legislator" who could persuade people to accept the rules necessary for such a society. Law in the properly constituted state would be, among other things, an instrument of transformation: "He who dares to undertake the making of a people's laws ought to feel himself capable of changing human nature." Rousseau had learned from the classical philosophers, however, that good laws can take root only amidst good customs. It was thus implicit in *The Social Contract* that many existing societies were already beyond help. "What people," Rousseau asked, "is a fit subject for legislation?" His answer was not encouraging to revolutionaries bent on overthrowing unjust regimes: "One which, already bound by some unity of origin, interest, or convention, has never yet felt the real yoke of law; . . . one in which every member may be known by every other, and there is no need to lay on any man burdens too heavy for a man to bear; . . . one which is neither rich nor poor, but self sufficient. . . . All these conditions are indeed rarely found united, and therefore few states have good constitutions."

Once a legitimate state is established, it needs to be maintained and defended. Thus, according to Rousseau, there should be no "particular associations" competing for the loyalty of citizens; religion should not be left independent of political control; and those who refuse to conform to the general will would have to be "forced to be free."

The contrast between Rousseau's program and the practical ideas that guided the American Founders could hardly be more striking. The legacy of the most influential political *thinker* of the eighteenth century is thus at odds with the era's greatest political *achievement* — the design for government framed by men who believed that good governments could be based on reflection and choice. The pragmatic authors of *The Federalist* had their own clear-eyed understanding of human nature with its potency and its limitations. They knew that human beings are creatures of reason and feeling — capable of good and evil, trust and betrayal, creativity and destruction, selfishness and cooperation. In Madison's famous formulation: "As there is a certain degree of depravity in human nature which requires a certain degree of circumspection and distrust, so there are other qualities in human nature which justify a certain portion of esteem and confidence."

As it turned out, Rousseau and his most discerning readers, especially Tocqueville, served the world's democratic experiments well as sources of constructive criticism. They were instrumental in keeping alive the classical insight that a healthy polity cannot be sustained without virtuous citizens and good customs. They have been among the main contributors to the classical critique of liberalism that has sustained, enriched, and corrected the excesses of democratic states. At the same time, however, liberal

democracy has been menaced by Rousseau's most illegitimate offspring —
not the Le Vasseurs who, God willing, are still thriving somewhere, but the
practitioners of the politics of feeling who bridle at authority themselves
but advocate authoritarian measures to force others to be free.

Generations of scholars have attempted to resolve the seeming contradictions in Rousseau's political writings, notably between his passionate attachment to natural freedom and his complacency about the state that forces
nonconformists to be free. Biographers have pointed out that Rousseau himself was against revolution; that he thought the ideas in *The Social Contract*
could work only in a small homogeneous polity like Geneva; and that he was
generally pessimistic about the possibility of changing bad institutions.

But in the worlds of politics and culture, what Rousseau actually said
or meant was of less consequence than the emotional responses his writings stirred. Rousseau's critique of existing governments was heady stuff.
The difficulty and subtlety of his political thought were masked by his
fluid, seductive literary style. His writings thus became a reservoir of ideas
and slogans from which individualists and communitarians, revolutionaries and conservatives, moralists and bohemians, constitutionalists and
Marxists drew freely and selectively. Vulgarization of his thought sheared
off his deep historical pessimism, with the result that his influence at the
popular level was overwhelmingly to the left where, ironically, it fed the
nineteenth-century cult of progress.

Though Rousseau can fairly be regarded as the leading secular thinker
of the Counter-Enlightenment, his "defense" of religion shows how firmly
he stood within the modern horizon of his antagonists, and how he extended that horizon. Voltaire and others, much impressed by the natural
science of their day, mounted an offensive against what they called "cleri-
calism" but by which they meant Christianity in general and Catholicism
in particular. They portrayed organized religion as an impediment to progress and a bastion of bigoted ignorance. Rousseau gained more credit than
he deserved for reproving their contempt of religion in his *First Discourse,*
for he was no friendlier to traditional religion than they. His childhood Calvinism and his brief, later passage through Catholicism left him with a vo-
cabulary and a critical stance, but little more. Where Christianity was concerned, he seems to have unquestioningly accepted the reigning opinion
among the secular learned men of his time.

He made his own views about organized religion clear in *Émile* and *The
Social Contract* — so clear in fact that he was forced to flee from both Swiss

and French authorities. The Savoyard vicar in *Émile* sounded much like Rousseau himself. He argued that the presence of religion in society should be welcomed, but not the religion of the day. Rejecting *both* reason and revelation, he proclaimed that "The essential worship is that of the heart. God does not reject its homage, if it is sincere, in whatever form it is offered to him." The religion that Rousseau "defended" was a radically subjective one, based on inner sentiment — a belief system rooted in being true to one's own feelings. It was the religion of Madame de Warens — the same religion that a U.S. Supreme Court plurality would one day attempt to establish when it announced a "right to define one's own concept of existence, of meaning, of the universe, and of the mystery of human life" (*Casey v. Planned Parenthood,* 1992).

That private, inner religion was well-suited for the ideal polity outlined in *The Social Contract.* Once a truly legitimate state has been constructed, Rousseau argued, religion would be helpful in shoring it up — ideally, a patriotic "civil religion." Sharing Hobbes's fear of competitors for loyalty with the state, Rousseau held that a well-constituted state could be tolerant of other sorts of religious activity so long as they remained inward and private. Unlike Luther and other reformers, he was uninterested in correcting the defects of institutional religion. He came not to support their critique, but to push it to the limit.

Morality, in Rousseau's view, was rooted in neither reason nor revelation, but in the natural feeling of compassion. Indeed, he is in an important sense the father of the politics of compassion. As we now know, however, compassion is a shaky foundation on which to build a just society. Compassion, unlike charity, is not a virtue acquired by self-discipline and habitual practice. It is only a feeling, and a fleeting one at that. It yields not only to self-preservation, but to self-interest.

Rousseau's thought won admiration from a surprising assortment of readers. *Julie* marked the rise of the romantic literary genre that celebrates the primacy of feeling and the beauties of nature, while the *Confessions* did the same for the modern literature of self-revelation. Taken out of context, his passages on the communal existence of peoples, his evocation of a lost happy childhood of the human race, and his stress on the importance of religion found wide and disparate audiences, as did his critiques of the commercial mentality, the institution of private property, and the conquest of nature. The new human sciences of anthropology and psychology and the modern understanding of history are all in his debt.

Yet not all of his insights were original. He borrowed heavily, though haphazardly, from classical and biblical sources to criticize the reigning dogmas of his age. The extent of his debt was not always apparent, for he was adept at "translating" traditional wisdom into language that appealed to secular intellectuals. Though his skepticism about the benefits of progress in the arts and sciences was at odds with widely held views among educated men of his time, such attitudes would have been common among the women who were his closest friends, and in popular devotional literature.

Madame de Stael once remarked of Rousseau, "He had nothing new, but he set everything on fire." Though exaggerating his lack of originality, she did not overestimate the magic of his prose. Rousseau was a consummate stylist, the father of the sound bite, a phrasemaker par excellence. Moreover, he gave many different kinds of readers the impression that he understood and empathized with their deepest concerns. Above all, he tapped into *ressentiment* as no writer had done before. All the humiliations he had suffered in his life, all the pettiness and vice he had observed in the households of the ruling classes, lent power to his prose. Many others before and since have written about the plight of the disadvantaged and the injuries of class, but Rousseau remains, as Judith Shklar neatly put it, the "Homer of the losers."

By Rousseau's own lights, however, his influence was different from, even opposite to, what he had hoped. His philosophical ideas, he frequently insisted, were only for the few, and the writings containing them could not be understood unless read in relation to one another — and more than once. The teaching of the *First Discourse,* for instance, is not that the sciences and the arts are unworthy pursuits, but that their spread to the public at large, their vulgarization, had had a corrupting effect — by destabilizing customary morality and fostering skepticism. The best education for ordinary folk, Rousseau held, was education aimed at the formation of healthy sentiments.

But no writer can control how and by whom his works are read. Discerning readers like Tocqueville and Kant were stimulated by Rousseau. To them, his writings were sources of enrichment and challenge, not least because, in his borderline mystical way, he carried forward to the new science of politics important insights from classical and biblical thought. Many activists who were "influenced" by Rousseau's political ideas, however, probably never read even one of his works in its entirety. More often than not, Rousseau's writings seem to have affected the emotions of his readers more than their intellects. Even Jacques Maritain, who detested Rousseau, conceded that, more than any other writer, Rousseau gave voice to the longings of his times:

> Such men are prophets of the spirit of the world, prophets of below, who concentrate in their heart the influences which work in the deeps of wounded humanity during a whole epoch. They then proclaim the age which is to follow them, and at the same time discharge on the future with prodigious strength those influences which have found their unity in them. They act on men by an awakening of emotional sympathies. . . . They spread around them the contagion of their self, the waves of their feelings and their instincts, they absorb people into their temperament.

What is one to make of a body of thought so ambiguous and so influential as that of Rousseau? Rousseau's native genius enabled him to acquire a good grasp of one of the two great premodern intellectual traditions. He learned enough from the ancient Greeks to mount a powerful critique of narrow scientific rationalism, but not enough to appreciate the more capacious form of reason that gave the classical and biblical traditions alike their dynamism. Like the Enlightenment thinkers he criticized, Rousseau rejected the moral and intellectual traditions that had nourished his own genius, throwing out the *ratio* of natural law along with modern scientific reason. He thus failed to see that what he called "perfectibility" was rooted in man's innate desire to know, the desire that gives rise to the never-ending, recurrent operations of questioning, experiencing, understanding, and choosing.

This prodigiously gifted, gravely flawed genius of the eighteenth century was at his best when he reminded his proud contemporaries of the limitations of science and politics. He sounded an early, much needed warning that material progress does not necessarily bring moral progress. He helped to keep alive the classical insight that good government requires moral foundations. He gave vivid expression to the plight of the poor and marginalized. But Rousseau's most problematic legacy, the one that bedevils us today, has been his elevation of sincerity over truth, and feeling over reason. Ironically, philosophical works he meant for the few fostered popular skepticism and relativism, while his writings addressed to the many promoted a revolt against reason even among philosophers.

Abraham Lincoln and the Last Best Hope

JEAN BETHKE ELSHTAIN

T HE BEGINNING OF THE NINTH CENTURY of the millennium now almost past was promising enough. The Congress of Vienna in 1815 marked, at long last, the end of the Napoleonic wars and heralded a period of enduring peace — peace under the auspices of emperors and monarchs of dubious legitimacy and stability, to be sure, but peace nonetheless. The settlement was far from complete. The Balkans remained a tinderbox and, indeed, the entire Austro-Hungarian Empire seemed an improbable thing to hold together indefinitely, composed as it was of a tension-ridden mix of languages, peoples, religions, and ethnic allegiances. Yet the Hapsburg crown, although loosely fixed on typically ineffectual royal heads, appeared more or less secure. In Russia, the Romanov autocracy was holding its own, despite rumblings of discontent connected, not least of all, with the continuing system of serfdom. France was — after Revolution, Terror, and Napoleon — a volatile mix of the autocratic and republican, but posed no immediate threat to others. The German-speaking peoples were scattered among multiple principalities, and spilled over into Russia, Central Europe, and — a point of major contention for France — Alsace-Lorraine. Only England appeared to have put together a workable combination of monarchy and constitutionalism.

The calendar notwithstanding, the real nineteenth century began in 1815, and the story of that century has often been depicted as one of Europe's outward expansion through territorial grabs ranging from Africa and Southeast Asia to the Indian subcontinent. Another story is that of "people's nationalism" within Europe, which erupted in the "springtime of the peoples" in 1848. Patriots such as Giuseppe Mazzini in Italy erected people's republics all over Europe, most of which were soon crushed by the old order. These reversals left in their aftermath nationalist frustrations that exploded sporadically — and most fatefully with the assassin's bullets that struck down Archduke Francis Ferdinand on June 28, 1914, precipitating the end of the century that began in 1815, and with it the end of the promise that was Europe.

But of course there was another nineteenth century, and there, too, promise and tragedy contended. A still young American republic strained outward in what seemed a limitless possibility of expansion driven by almost every human passion imaginable — ambition, greed, patriotism, desperation, curiosity, and a simple desire to better one's lot. Whatever the western pioneers were looking for, they usually found hard work and, for those with a little luck and the toughness to stick with it, a modest reward. It was a hard-scrabble frontier existence into which, on February 12, 1809, was born the figure who is at the center of the ninth reflection in this millennium series. So very much has been written about him, and I'm not sure that I, or anyone else for that matter, can say much that is new. But one need never apologize for thinking again about Abraham Lincoln.

Thomas Lincoln had managed to scrape together enough money to buy a small tract in Kentucky, and, as his son would later write, they moved when he was still a little boy to a larger tract "in the valley of Knob Creek, surrounded by high hills and deep gorges." It was rocky, unfruitful soil where the furious washing of a "big rain in the hills" would sweep new planting "clear off the field." The American frontier was called a new world, but it was a peasant subsistence very much like what had been known for centuries in the old. It seems that the mother, Nancy Hanks Lincoln, was able to read but could not write. Life was nonstop work from dawn to dusk, and "book learning" was held in slight regard.

Separating as best we can fact from legend, we know that the Lincolns set out for Indiana in 1816, crossing the Ohio River in search of better land titles and — at least according to recent biographer David Herbert Donald — in order to get away from slavery. Thomas Lincoln, who favored the Separate Baptist Church, apparently opposed slavery on both religious and economic grounds. Slave labor, he believed, was unfair competition to "free labor," and that argument was carried forward by Abraham, who was a free labor advocate throughout his years as a Whig and, later, as a Republican. From his mother's early death, it is said, began the spells of melancholia that would never leave him. In 1817 she succumbed to what was called "milk sickness," and a year later was succeeded by a stepmother, Sarah, who trailed in her wake three children and elegant domestic furnishings, such as were previously unknown to the Lincoln household. Sarah's liveliness did not end young Abraham's descents into melancholy, but we are told that the ungainly youth became sprightlier. Although Sarah was illiterate, Lincoln was now introduced to schooling for the first time, which quickly sparked his famous passion for book learning.

Lincoln's education, which may strike us as haphazard, was largely a matter of being drilled in the basics of grammar, spelling, composition, and ciphering, as it was called. Donald notes that Lincoln's contemporaries "attributed prodigies of reading to him, but books were scarce on the frontier and he had to read carefully rather than extensively. He memorized a great deal of what he read." Today, of course, memorization is routinely dismissed as "rote learning," and priority is given to "self-expression" in the service of "authenticity" and other presumed goods. Reflecting on the experience of Lincoln (and innumerable others subjected to "rote learning") may lead one to suspect that there is much to be said for having one's mind formed by the best that others have thought and said before giving it unbridled expression. All those hours spent reading by dim firelight the same book over and over (the way little children still like to be read to) were to contribute to Lincoln's being the foremost master of prose among our presidents. Indeed, he has few peers in our entire history.

For young Lincoln, as for so many others of the time, an inescapable book was John Bunyan's *Pilgrim's Progress,* first published in 1678. It is difficult for us today to appreciate the pervasive power and influence of Bunyan's tale, told "in the similitude of a Dream." In that sustained religious allegory of moral heroism and imagery both vivid and frightening, the reader lives through Christian's travails and all-too-human backsliding, until finally tasting his victory as one's own. Bunyan's biting commentary on human folly, joined to an inspiring account of human possibility, must have played an important part in shaping Lincoln's complexity of mind through a life of action and of reflection, often mordant reflection, on that action.

With the teenage years, Lincoln set out to escape the hard life he had known and became something of a drifter — trying on, as it were, different tasks, vocations, and identities. Settling in New Salem, Illinois, he took up the practice of law and began "politicking." The Lincoln legend has this "fresh breeze from off the prairie" (as Jane Addams called him) going from splitting rails to the White House, but neglects the many years in between when he was refining his craft as a speaker, writer, and politician. Despite distractions, setbacks, and uncertainties, his course was steadily upward: the move to Springfield, marriage with Mary Todd, election to the state legislature. As a politician he was mainly preoccupied with routine questions of domestic improvements, currency, and contract law. He was, in short, the familiar Whig politician, although a Whig with a growing reputation for straightforwardness, rough-hewn honesty, mental agility (with a streak of ironic humor), and a capacity for getting things done.

On the great question, Lincoln had never been pro-slavery, but his early pronouncements addressed it almost entirely in terms of free labor. Importing slaves into the new territories, he contended, would create unfair competition for non-slave labor. Under the force of circumstances and his own reflection, however, his public statements slowly began to change. The great question heated up with the passage of the Kansas-Nebraska Act of 1854, which opened the western territories to slavery. The question was being recast in terms of a constitutional and moral crisis, with Northern calls for emancipation becoming ever more adamant. In response, Lincoln delivered a speech in Peoria, Illinois, on October 16, 1854, that may fairly be said to have put him on the course to his place in history.

He acknowledged the extraordinary difficulties in extirpating an established social institution, even when that institution is as pernicious as slavery. He allowed that his Southern contemporaries had not created the institution, and that "it is very difficult to get rid of it, in any satisfactory way." His own preference was to "free all the slaves, and send them to Liberia," but he knew the "sudden execution" of such a plan to be "impossible." Even if it were possible to send all the slaves there, most of them would likely perish without a means of support. Also unacceptable, he said, is the alternative of freeing the slaves and then keeping them here as "underlings." Because of a "universal feeling, whether well- or ill-founded" (a feeling that Lincoln confessed he shared), the option of making freed slaves "politically and socially our equals" was also excluded. His position was that slaves did have constitutional rights that must be respected, "not grudgingly, but fully and fairly." This left him with the proposal that the best to be done at present was to prevent the extension of slavery and to look forward to the possibility of "gradual emancipation." Even in the Peoria speech that gained him national attention, however, he left no doubt that his opposition to Kansas-Nebraska was based on the conviction that the "new free states are places for poor people to go to and better their condition." He frankly admitted that his chief concern was the welfare of poor whites.

Readers today may think the speech tepid, even repugnantly cautious. This is no clarion call for abolition. It is a thoughtful reflection on the relationship between moral duty and political possibility in the recognition that the two are not always nicely matched. Yet in the same speech he declared that there is no "moral right in the enslaving of one man by another." Slavery is a form of theft that violates the basic principle that none should live by the fruits of another's forced labor. In a manner both earthy and clear, Lincoln preached a "labor theory of value" not entirely unlike the theory advanced with such obtuse complexity by Karl Marx. He draws on a naturalistic morality, not entirely unlike natural law, rather than invoking doctrines of revealed religion. Slavery, he believed, is a consequence of our most base natural drives and is incompatible with a "love of justice" that is also natural. First principles are involved, and those principles can be known through reason. In 1858 he wrote a three-sentence summary of his thought "On Slavery and Democracy": "As I would not be a *slave,* so I would not be a *master.* This expresses my idea of democracy. Whatever differs from this, to the extent of the difference, is no democracy."

To the extent that it countenanced the institution of slavery, it would seem to follow, his country was not a democracy. Lincoln did not reach that conclusion lightly, such was his piety toward the American Founders. But he came to the view that their preeminent task had been to forge the federal union. They had no choice but to leave the slavery question to a future generation — to his generation. In this way of thinking, the Framers had not resolved but had only postponed the question of slavery, and Lincoln's sense that the time had come to move, however cautiously, toward a resolution had about it a force of obligation that he did not hesitate to call sacred.

In his 1858 debates with Stephen Douglas, the argument is extended: Slavery is not only wrong, it also "threatens the Union." While Lincoln continued to play to the race fears that were part of the free labor platform, he was also clear on what should have to give when popular sovereignty clashes with moral right. His devotion to democracy did not include the idolatrous doctrine that the voice of the people is the voice of God. What is true for the voice of the people applied also to the voice of courts. By ruling that slaves had no rights that white men were required to respect, the infamous Dred Scott decision of 1857, said Lincoln, was responsible for "blowing out the moral lights." The "real issue in this controversy," he contended against Douglas, is slavery and whether it should be treated as a "moral, social, and political wrong" or whether it should be made "perpetual and national."

While Lincoln lost the senatorial election of 1858, his campaign laid the foundation for his nomination and election as president in 1860. It was now clear to him that his task was the "repurifying" of the republic, to cleanse it "in the spirit, if not the blood, of the Revolution." "Let us," he declared, "re-adopt the Declaration of Independence, and with it, the practices and policy which harmonize with it." He had accused Douglas of distorting the views of the Founders; there is not, he insisted, a shred of evidence that "the Negro was not included in the Declaration of Independence." That being said, the new president was not at all clear about what was to be done — meaning what was to be done without spilling rivers of blood and abandoning the American experiment in self-government.

The debate over the Civil War and Lincoln's part in precipitating, pursuing, and concluding it will continue as long as the American republic. That conflict is our defining tragedy. Yet Lincoln's words and conduct as war leader and definer of the conflict runs against the usual definition of the American character. He never minimized the costs or exaggerated what the war would achieve; his language was at once prophetic and tragic. If the defining American myth is that of Progress, the belief that each new time will be an improvement over what went before, Lincoln did not subscribe to it. He resisted also the temptation to depict opponents as wholly evil while casting oneself and one's allies as the "children of light." Much of American politics has been in the mode of moral crusade. Earlier in this century we fought a war to end all wars and make the world safe for democracy. The prohibition of liquor promised a nation restored to righteousness. Women's suffrage was not a matter of simple justice but what Elizabeth Cady Stanton called a "new evangel of womanhood." Examples of the crusading credo in action can readily be multiplied.

In *the* great conflict of American history, Lincoln seems almost unAmerican in his refusal to embrace that credo. A terrible duty had to be done and a terrible price had to be paid, and, in doing that duty and paying that price, good and evil were to be found on both sides of the conflict. In his resistance to the pattern of American "triumphalism," it is not too much to say that Lincoln reflected an Augustinian perspective on the ambiguities of history. Politics is a severely limited instrument, and the task of bringing about a social order approximately more just is always an unfinished task. All this is evident, above all, in Lincoln's own words — words that American schoolchildren, at least outside the deep South, were once required to memorize. Lincoln's words bear the weight of his awareness that he was, in ways not of his own desire or design, authoring and thereby authorizing the future of a republic "purified" by the blood of both North and South. Purified of the great wrong of slavery but not yet, perhaps not ever, pure.

The sense of dedication to an unfinished task comes through most powerfully in the Gettysburg Address. As all know, the featured speaker of the day was Edward Everett, the most famous orator of the time, a spellbinder who took two hours to say the many things appropriate to say upon the dedication of a military cemetery. Not until many years later did the public pay much attention to the few words of the president that followed. "Fourscore and seven years ago," and then it was "shall not perish from the earth," and the president had sat down before many in the crowd realized he was speaking. Those few words, barely mentioned at the time in the inside pages of the newspapers, have likely occasioned more reflection than any other text among people who would understand the genius of the American experiment. He spoke of consecration and hallowing, of a new birth of freedom and of a nation under God, but all without explicit reference to Divine agency or scriptural text. There is no doubt about the piety, but it is not piety on parade.

Setting aside the much discussed question of Lincoln's religion, there can be no doubt about his deep immersion in the cadences and parables of the Bible. His impatience with those who presumed to know the purposes of God has frequently been remarked. The proper human stance before the ways of the Lord, he believed, is that of deep humility. Thus he writes to Albert G. Hodges on April 4, 1864, a year before his own death, "I claim not to have controlled events, but confess plainly that events have controlled me." American political historian John Diggins says that Lincoln helped heal the "Machiavellian wound" that resulted from the separation of politics and morality. Lincoln, he believes, renewed the theory of statecraft by insisting that "ultimate moral questions did not admit of relativistic interpretations," while knowing at the same time that the attempt to right moral wrongs may have tragic consequences and almost certainly will not achieve unqualified success.

But again, our best course is to attend to the words of Lincoln. Recall the Second Inaugural Address of March 4, 1865, little more than a month before his death. There are two paragraphs on the war and the imperative to save the Union, moving directly in the next paragraph, the heart of the speech, to slavery. One side, he observes, wanted to strengthen and perpetuate the institution, the other to restrict its enlargement. (And, although he does not say so, many on the Northern side were determined to abolish it.) In any event, nobody expected a war of such magnitude and duration. Each hoped for an "easier triumph, and a result less fundamental and astounding." Then come the extraordinary words that better educated Americans know almost by heart:

Both read the same Bible, and pray to the same God; and each invokes His aid against the other. It may seem strange that any men should dare to ask a just God's assistance in wringing their bread from the sweat of other men's faces; but let us judge not that we be not judged. The prayers of both could not be answered; that of neither has been answered fully. The Almighty has His own purposes. "Woe unto the world because of offenses; for it must needs be that offenses come, but woe to that man by whom the offense cometh!" If we shall suppose that American slavery is one of those offenses which, in the providence of God, must needs come, but which, having continued through His appointed time, He now wills to remove, and that He gives to both North and South this terrible war as the woe due to those by whom the offense came, shall we discern therein any departure from those divine attributes which the believers in a living God always ascribe to Him?

The form changes now to that of supplication:

Fondly do we hope — fervently do we pray — that this mighty scourge of war may speedily pass away. Yet, if God wills that it continue, until all the wealth piled up by the bondsman's two hundred and fifty years of unrequited toil shall be sunk, and until every drop of blood drawn with the lash shall be paid by another drawn with the sword, as was said three thousand years ago, so still it must be said, "The judgments of the Lord are true and righteous altogether."

Of course, Southerners would for generations deride these words as an indulgence in unctuous self-righteousness, and it is obvious that Lincoln was not "above" the conflict he is discussing. The description of the conflict is not, as it is said today, nonpartisan. His duty, reluctantly accepted, had been to be a partisan and a leader of partisans, but the import of the address is that now that time is past. More remarkable in the words of a victorious party is the refusal to recruit God as a partisan. The war and its outcome do not vindicate a grand narrative of historical inevitability but bring all parties under Divine judgment. We are united as a bleeding and wounded people, and it is on the basis of that experience, not on victory parades and rallies, that a nation is to be renewed. With Augustine, Lincoln recognized the lust to dominate that is so inextricably entangled with yearnings for peace and justice. No one walks away even from a justifiable war morally unscathed.

Lincoln offers words that are, at the same time, benediction, his own epitaph, and a continuing inspiration to a more worthy politics.

> With malice toward none, with charity for all, with firmness in the right as God gives us to see the right, let us strive on to finish the work we are in, to bind up the nation's wounds, to care for him who shall have borne the battle and for his widow and his orphan, to do all which may achieve and cherish a just and a lasting peace among ourselves and with all nations.

The reference to other nations is by no means incidental to Lincoln's understanding of what was at stake in America's conflict. In history's ongoing struggle between despotism and self-government, he was prepared to believe that America was earth's "last best hope" — not as the world's economic colossus or imperial hegemon but as an exemplar of what politics, with all its limitations, can accomplish.

A poem to which Lincoln often returned was "Oh, Why Should the Spirit of Mortal Be Proud?" written by one William Knox. Forget that it is not great poetry, indeed that it descends to doggerel. It says something important about the man who thought it wise.

> Oh, why should the spirit of mortal be proud?
> Like a swift fleeting meteor, a fast-flying cloud,
> A flash of the lightning, a break of the wave,
> Man passeth from life to his rest in the grave. . . .

The hand of the king that the sceptre hath borne;
The brow of the priest that the mitre hath worn;
The eye of the sage and the heart of the brave,
Are hidden and lost in the depth of the grave. . . .

The saint who enjoyed the communion of heaven,
The sinner who dared to remain unforgiven,
The wise and the foolish, the guilty and just,
Have quietly mingled their bones in the dust. . . .

'Tis the wink of an eye, 'tis the draught of a breath,
From the blossom of health to the paleness of death,
From the gilded saloon to the bier and the shroud —
Oh, why should the spirit of mortal be proud?

Perhaps it is too obvious to observe that, in an era of sound bites, poll-driven politicians, plausible deniability, single-interest PACs, and media spinmeisters, Lincoln seems to exist in a different moral and political universe. And it is both true and a very good thing that other presidents did not have such momentous events by which they were controlled and made candidates for comparable greatness. That being said, however, Lincoln is by no means irrelevant. He was in most respects a politician like other politicians. He knew all about interests and power, was a master of clever ripostes, well-placed barbs, and the tricks of outwitting opponents. In short, he played the game and played it very well.

The difference is that he never forgot that politics is one way in which very imperfect human beings can enact projects based on moral reasoning; that politics is a theater of both comedy and tragedy, relentless in the teaching of humility. It is cause for both amazement and gratitude that, in a century when the promise of Europe migrated to a New World which, or so we are told, offers the prospect of the nearest thing there has ever been to a universal history of freedom and justice, Abraham Lincoln was president of these United States of America. More than a hundred years later, there is no point in hoping for another Abraham Lincoln. But one may hope that we have not entirely forgotten the possibilities of political and moral leadership that he exemplified.

John Paul II and the Crisis of Humanism

GEORGE WEIGEL

As *Time* and other premillennial makers of lists have discovered in recent months, there is no lack of candidates for the position of emblematic figure of the twentieth century.

In the world of politics alone, there are several plausible nominees on a slate that includes the admirable and the odious in fairly equal proportion: Churchill, Lenin, Stalin, Mao, Roosevelt, Reagan. Widening the search beyond the world of organized political power, a powerful case can be made for James Watson and Francis Crick, unravelers of the DNA "double-helix," the key to biotechnology and what will almost certainly be the most urgent set of issues on the twenty-first century's public agenda. In a historical period dramatically shaped by the application, for good or ill, of new scientific knowledge, some might also argue for Fermi, Heisenberg, or another of the great mid-century nuclear physicists as the man who made the most enduring impact on our times. And while his status as a scientist and a student of the human condition has been badly shaken in recent decades, there is no doubt that Sigmund Freud had an enormous impact on the twentieth century.

There is an element of the arbitrary in all such list making, of course. And indeed here is an instance where the postmodern passion for hermeneutics makes eminent sense. In choosing the emblematic figure of the century now drawing rapidly to a close, it really is a matter of how one looks at things — in this instance, the dynamics of history.

If one believes that politics is not an independent variable in human affairs — if politics is a function of culture, and at the heart of culture is *cultus,* religion, what we cherish and what we worship — then a serious case can be made for Pope John Paul II as the man who most singularly embodies humanity's trials and triumphs in the twentieth century.

One facet of the "culture first" case for John Paul II's preeminence is institutional. The Roman Catholic Church has arguably been the most influential religious community of the past ten decades in shaping the world the twenty-first century will inherit; the Catholic Church has been decisively formed for the next century by John Paul's authoritative interpretation of the Second Vatican Council, the most important religious event of *this* century; therefore John Paul II can be considered the twentieth century's seminal figure. Moreover, his teachings will be institutionally developed and carried into the future, unlike another great Slavic moral witness with a plausible claim to being the man of the century, Aleksandr Solzhenitsyn. In making that case, of course, it has to be remembered that a great reforming Pope and his accomplishments are not an individual achievement. John Paul II emerged from the heart of the Church and the priesthood, and he cannot be understood apart from that.

But a deeper argument can and should be explored here. John Paul II is not the emblematic figure of the twentieth century simply because his teachings and witness, which have had such a demonstrable impact on the history of our times, will be institutionally extended into the future, unlike the teachings of Churchill, Lenin, Stalin, Mao, FDR, or Reagan. No, John Paul II is arguably *the* iconic figure of the twentieth century because his life has embodied, personally and spiritually, the human crises with which Churchill, Lenin, Stalin, Mao, FDR, and Reagan (not to mention Watson and Crick, Heisenberg, Fermi, and Freud) were all engaged in their distinctive ways. And his teaching, which has emerged from a profound philosophical and theological reflection on those crises, has demonstrated the resilience, indeed the indispensability, of religious conviction in addressing the crisis of contemporary humanism. The twentieth century, which began with the confident assertion that a maturing humanity had outgrown its "need" for religion, proved that men could indeed organize the world without God. It also proved that, in doing so, men could only organize the world against each other, bringing humanity to the brink of catastrophe on more than one occasion.

Finally, if one believes that the Christian movement bears the truth of the world's story, then John Paul II looms very large indeed. So, of course, do others: Billy Graham, who gave a new dynamism and unprecedented worldwide reach to evangelical Protestantism; Karl Barth, embodiment of the last great effort within the sixteenth-century Reformation traditions to reconstitute Christian orthodoxy apart from Rome or the Christian East. But neither Graham nor Barth became the kind of global moral witness that John Paul II has become. And in that sense (for the Pope insists that his public moral witness is, *semper et ubique,* a function of his Christian faith), neither was the kind of evangelist that John Paul II has been, throughout the worlds-within-worlds of humanity.

Nineteen sixty-eight was a bad year in a century replete with bad years. In February of the year in which the West seemed to come apart at the seams and Red Army tanks crushed the reform communism of the Prague Spring, Cardinal Karol Wojtyla of Krakow wrote his friend, the Jesuit theologian Henri de Lubac, about the large-scale philosophical project on which he was engaged in the midst of his pastoral responsibilities:

> I devote my very rare free moments to a work that is close to my heart and devoted to the metaphysical sense and mystery of the person. It seems to me that the debate today is being played out on that level. The evil of our times consists in the first place in a kind of degradation, indeed in a pulverization, of the fundamental uniqueness of each human person. This evil is even more of the metaphysical order than of the moral order. To this disintegration planned at times by atheistic ideologies we must oppose, rather than sterile polemics, a kind of "recapitulation" of the inviolable mystery of the person.

That radical humanism — that life-forming commitment to "the inviolable mystery of the person" — was, and is, Karol Wojtyla's response to a century in which false humanisms had created mountains of corpses and an ocean of blood, Auschwitz and the Gulag, abortion as a widespread means of fertility regulation, and the prospect of the biotechnical remanufacture of the *humanum.* In thinking through, preaching, writing about, and acting upon the implications of a radical humanism worthy of the human person, John Paul II addressed three of the most pressing issues on the human agenda in a way that seems likely to shape the debate on those issues long into the future: the priority of culture, the nature of sexual love, and the anthropology of freedom.

In the first instance, he boldly challenged the notion, rampant throughout the century, that either politics or economics was the engine of world-historical change.

The twentieth century experienced the lethal consequences of the political madnesses set loose in the world by the French Revolution. And this made it all the more striking (and perhaps indicative of the divine sense of irony) that the collapse of totalitarianism as a plausible political model came in 1989, two hundred years after the Jacobin fire had first melted men's minds and consciences in the name of a false idea of freedom. Marxist economics would have engineered its own failure in due course, given its evident incapacity to compete in a world dominated by the microchip and digital revolutions. But even after communism was on the wane — indeed, even after its collapse — a kind of Marxist hangover continued in the West, where too many continued to believe that economics rules reality.

John Paul II's role in the collapse of European communism rid his Slavic brethren of that particular political plague, challenged the assumed preeminence of politics and economics in our understanding of history, and taught the world a lesson about the real engine of change: culture.

The Pope's pilgrimages to Poland in June 1979 and to Cuba in January 1998 were the two bookends, so to speak, of his "culture first" strategy of change, which is the public dimension of his long-standing commitment to resist the "pulverization" of the human person (as he put it to de Lubac). In both Poland and Cuba, Communist regimes had held a historically Christian nation in their grip for forty years. In both Poland and Cuba, John Paul addressed that particular political form of human pulverization by restoring to a people its authentic history and cultural memory. His message said, in various ways and without ever making reference to the regime then in power, "You are not who they say you are. Here is who you are. You [Poles, Cubans] are 'Polish' [or 'Cuban'] because Christianity was the crucial factor in creating a human reality called 'Poles' [or 'Cubans']. Reclaim that source of your identity, deepen your commitment to it, and you will be free in a way that no worldly power can ever take from you." The results were evident in Poland within fourteen months: a revolution of conscience, launched by John Paul II in June 1979, gave birth in Gdansk to the Solidarity movement, and ten years of nonviolent struggle later, communism was finished. The results have not been as rapid or dramatic in Cuba, but Fidel Castro and those who would continue his style of governance cannot be optimistic about the ultimate outcome.

The crack-up of communism was, like all epic historical moments, the product of the convergence of many things: Marxism's economic inadequacies; the dynamics let loose in east central Europe by the 1975 Helsinki Final Act; the policies of Ronald Reagan and Margaret Thatcher; generational change in the Soviet leadership. But if one wants to understand *why* communism collapsed when it did (in 1989, rather than in 1999, or 2009, or 2019) and *how* it did (without bloodshed, in the main), then one simply must factor into this complex equation John Paul II's revolution of conscience. And in taking account of that, one is inoculated against both the Jacobin-political and Marxist-economic delusions about the dynamics of history. For that epic achievement alone, John Paul II has a serious claim to being considered the emblematic figure of his, and our, times.

Then there was, and is, the sexual revolution, another attempt to redefine the humanum in the name of a certain concept of freedom: in this instance, the freedom to pursue the pleasure principle so long as "no one else" (or no one else in whom the state asserts a "compelling interest") gets hurt. World Christianity's early response to the sexual revolution was not impressive. Much of liberal Protestantism simply surrendered to it. And the 1968 encyclical *Humanae Vitae,* the first major papal attempt to address the implications of the sexual revolution after it had broken out into mainstream Western culture, was a pastoral failure. When John Paul II was elected ten years later, the *Humanae Vitae* episode had contributed to a serious credibility problem for the Church on a host of other, related issues; and, just at the moment when the human wreckage caused by the sexual revolution had begun to cause some second thoughts among its former enthusiasts (especially among women), the Catholic Church, it seemed, had little to contribute to restructuring the argument.

John Paul II's "theology of the body," which he laid out in 130 general audience addresses between 1979 and 1984, is arguably the most creative Christian response to the sexual revolution and its "pulverization" of the human person to be articulated in the twentieth century. Its philosophical core is Wojtyla's claim that what we might call a "Law of the Gift" is built into the very structure of human being-in-the-world. Because of that, self-giving, not self-assertion, is the royal road to human flourishing.

This depth truth of the human condition, which John Paul believed could be demonstrated by a careful analysis of human moral agency, had enormous implications for meeting the challenge of the sexual revolution. Sex, as often experienced in today's sexual free-fire zone, is instinctive and impersonal. But that kind of sex does not rise above the level of animal sexuality, which is also instinctive and impersonal. Sex that is an expression of self-giving love, not a use of the other for temporary gratification, is the only sex worthy of human beings. Chastity, on this analysis, is what John Paul called the "integrity of love," the virtue that makes it possible for one to love another as a *person.* We are made free, Wojtyla argues, so that we can make a free gift of ourselves to others; we are free so that we can love freely, and thus love truly. Genuine freedom — the freedom that disposes of itself in self-giving — is the context of a genuinely humanistic sexual ethic.

The theological core of John Paul's "theology of the body" is his profoundly sacramental apprehension of reality. Our embodiedness as male and female is not an accident of evolutionary biology, he insists. Rather, that embodiedness and the mutuality built into it express some of the deepest truths of the world, and teach us something about the world's Creator. John Paul even goes so far as to propose that sexual love within the bond of marital fidelity is an icon of the interior life of God the Holy Trinity, a community of mutual self-donation and mutual receptivity. Thus sexual love, within the bond of Christian marriage, is an act of worship.

It will be well into the twenty-first century before the Catholic Church, much less the wider culture, even begins to assimilate the contents of John Paul II's theology of the body. A secondary literature capable of unpacking these dense, compact audience addresses is badly needed. But for the moment, it is worth noting that the Bishop of Rome, often assumed to be the custodian of a tradition deeply scarred by a Manichean deprecation of human sexuality, has articulated a deeply humanistic response to the sexual revolution that says to the readers of *Playboy* and *Cosmopolitan* alike, "Human sexuality is far greater than you imagine."

In the third place, John Paul II's radical humanism has helped recast the debate about the future of public life in free societies for the twenty-first century. After a century in which monarchy had collapsed and totalitarianism in its Fascist and Communist forms had been defeated, it seemed at the opening of the 1990s as if democracy and the market were triumphant. If you wanted a society that protected basic human rights while advancing the common good, you chose the participatory politics of democracy; if you wanted economic growth, a higher material standard of living for all, and the widest possible inclusion in what Richard John Neuhaus has called the "circle of productivity and exchange," you chose a market-oriented, not state-directed, economy. John Paul II shared both of those convictions, as he made clear in the 1991 encyclical *Centesimus Annus*. But he quickly decoded the new threats to the "mystery of the human person" in the post–Cold War world, and he spent much of the decade of the 1990s trying to explain that freedom detached from moral truth — the "freedom of indifference" that dominated the high culture of the triumphant West — was, inevitably, self-cannibalizing.

Freedom untethered from truth is freedom's worst enemy. For if there is only your truth and my truth, and neither one of us recognizes a transcendent moral standard (call it "*the* truth") by which to adjudicate our differences, then the only way to settle the argument is for you to impose your power on me, or for me to impose my power on you. Freedom untethered from truth leads to chaos; chaos leads to anarchy; and since human beings cannot tolerate anarchy, tyranny as the answer to the human imperative of order is just around the corner. The false humanism of the freedom of indifference leads first to freedom's decay, and then to freedom's demise.

Similarly, on the economic front, unless a vibrant public moral culture disciplines and directs the explosive human energies let loose by the free market, the market ends up destroying the culture that makes it possible. In what Zbigniew Brzezinski nicely described as the "permissive cornucopia" of the future, a society of unprecedented material wealth and equally unprecedented license, the virtues necessary for the market to work — self-command, the willingness to defer gratification, the talent for teamwork, the skill of prudent risk-taking — atrophy. MTV, not the Federal Trade Commission or the International Monetary Fund, is the true enemy of the free economy.

This vision of the free, prosperous, *and virtuous* society, itself a product of the radical humanism of Karol Wojtyla, has not won the day in the developed world. But the proposal is out there. And that proposal is part of the intellectual and moral patrimony of over a billion Roman Catholics, as well as many, many others who find in it the most comprehensive, and compelling vision of public life on offer at the threshold of a new century and a new millennium. That proposal, too, buttresses the claim that Pope John Paul II is the emblematic man of our times.

"Be not afraid!", the antiphon of John Paul's inaugural homily on October 22, 1978, quickly became a kind of motto for the pontificate. That this clarion call to a recovery of courage at the end of the twentieth century was never regarded, even by the Pope's adversaries, as an impossible dream or a sentimental piety tells us a lot about Karol Wojtyla. Milovan Djilas (then a dissident in what was then Yugoslavia) was right when he said that the most impressive thing about the Pope was that he was a man utterly without fear. Courage of that sort explains a good part of the attraction of Karol Wojtyla's radical humanism as a response to the crises of the twentieth century.

It is just as important, however, to underline that this fearlessness is neither Stoic in character nor the by-product of Karol Wojtyla's personal "autonomy." Rather, it is a specifically Christian fearlessness. It was first exemplified for young Karol Wojtyla by his widower-father and by the bishop who ordained him, the man he calls the "unbroken prince," Cardinal Adam Stefan Sapieha, who led the Church of Krakow through the dark night of the Nazi Occupation. Those experiences of fearlessness have been deepened by Wojtyla's lifelong meditation on the mystery of the Cross, for the Pope is, in his heart, a Carmelite, and St. John of the Cross remains his spiritual master. His Cross-centered gaze on the world and its history precludes any hint of the Panglossian in the Pope's Christian humanism. In it, fear is not displaced, but rather transformed: transformed through a deep personal encounter with the crucified and abandoned Christ, which sets those who experience it free from fear.

That the universality of one's interests, compassion, and concerns is in inverse proportion to the depth of one's particular convictions is one of the truisms of the late twentieth century. By the general reckoning of many of his contemporaries, the intensity of Karol Wojtyla's conviction that the Cross is the truth of the world, and not simply another option in a supermarket of "spiritualities," ought to have made him an impossibly narrow, even dangerous, sectarian. But here, too, Pope John Paul II has been an important, perhaps even decisive, sign of contradiction.

Judged by externals, John Paul II has a claim to papal greatness and to world attention because of the exceptional range of his outreach to those who do not share his deepest convictions: to secular scientists, to Jews, to Muslims, to Christians of other confessions. Yet Wojtyla insists that these encounters (which, in the case of the dialogue with Judaism, are of a sort not seen for more than nineteen hundred years) have come about not despite his Christian faith but because of it. Respectful dialogue with all who are "other" is not in tension with Christian orthodoxy or the papal task of safeguarding the deposit of faith. Respectful encounter and dialogue are what Christian orthodoxy demands.

The Pope himself was eager to make this point at the United Nations in 1995. In a passage that surprised some observers because it invoked what one official in the Vatican Secretariat of State called the "J-word" before an audience of world political leaders, John Paul made sure that everyone present in the General Assembly hall knew that his defense of universal human rights and a genuine humanism for the post–Cold War world was not the result of some generic "spirituality." Defining himself as a "witness to hope," the Pope had this to say about the sources of that hope and its public implications:

> As a Christian, my hope and trust are centered on Jesus Christ, the two thousandth anniversary of whose birth will be celebrated at the coming of the new millennium. . . . *Jesus Christ is for us God made man, and made part of the history of humanity. Precisely for this reason, Christian hope for the world and its future extends to every human person.* Because of the radiant humanity of Christ, nothing genuinely human fails to touch the hearts of Christians. Faith in Christ does not impel us to intolerance. On the contrary, it obliges us to engage in a respectful dialogue. Love of Christ does not distract us from interest in others, but rather invites us to responsibility for them, to the exclusion of no one. . . . Thus as we approach the two thousandth anniversary of the birth of Christ, the Church asks only to be able to propose respectfully this message of salvation, and to be able to promote, in charity and service, the solidarity of the entire human family.

He was standing at the marble rostrum of the UN General Assembly, but he was teaching a basic lesson in Christology. And in doing so, the Pope was calling both Christians and those for whom Christianity is ineluctably "sectarian" because of its insistence on the universal salvific mission of Christ to take seriously the central Christian doctrine of the Incarnation.

It was not the first time John Paul had addressed this issue or suggested that it had important public implications. In *Redemptoris Missio*, his 1990 encyclical on Christian mission, John Paul had taught the orthodox faith of the Church: that many are saved who do not belong to the Church, but that those who are not saved in the Church are nonetheless saved because of Christ. At the same time, and in the same encyclical, John Paul made a decisive break with certain aspects of the Christian past and embraced the method of freedom when he wrote that *"The Church proposes; she imposes nothing"* (emphasis in original). Here was a decisive, historic break with the shadow-side of the Constantinian legacy. The Church, not by a merely prudential calculus but for the weightiest of theological reasons, renounced any use of state power in advancing its mission. A deep respect for every human being's search for the truth and a commitment to the method of persuasion in preaching the gospel were twin, "universal" implications of the radical specificity of the Christian claim embedded in the doctrine of the Incarnation.

And here, too, John Paul II taught the twentieth century something important about the nature of the human person and about genuine humanism. A universal empathy with others comes through, not around, particular convictions. One empirical test of the truth of particular convictions is their capacity to engage empathetically with the "other" in ways that enrich the humanity of all concerned. It was, in the root meaning of the word, a crucial lesson at the end of a century in which "otherness" had too often been seen as a lethal threat, with lethal consequences.

The twentieth century, which witnessed the announcement of the death of God, was in fact a century of the death of the gods. None of the false gods of the twentieth century was able to exorcise the paralyzing fear that first hung like a pall over the opening battles of World War I and then drifted down the decades, blighting the lives and destinies of four generations of human beings. Being on the right side of history didn't expel the demon of fear from the Bolsheviks and their progeny; it gave greater scope to deviltry, from the execution rooms in the Lubyanka basement to the frozen wastelands of the Kolyma mines. Racial determinism and its presumption of biological superiority didn't exorcise the passions that informed German National Socialism; the master race, living out its fears, created a new reign of terror from the Atlantic to the Urals. The therapeutic society explained fear away, which worked only for a while, or medicated it, which was another form of the pulverization of the human person.

In the face of the great fear of his time — a fear formed by irrationality and the nihilism that always accompanies the degradation of reason — John Paul II could say, and mean, "Be not afraid!" because he worshiped the one true God, whose conquest of fear he had encountered in God's only-begotten Son.

With the incarnation of Jesus of Nazareth, a human being was inextricably taken up into the Godhead. And if, as St. Paul insisted to the Romans,

Jesus Christ is the firstfruits of God's salvific action in and for the world, then all creation is eschatologically destined to fulfillment within the inner life of God. This truly radical humanism is the most compelling response to the false humanisms that wrought havoc with the twentieth century. Communion with God is the source of the liberation that humanism has sought for centuries.

John Paul himself would insist most vigorously that there are many others who could claim to be the human icon of the twentieth century. This is not simply a question of modesty, for Pope John Paul II knows that the truths he has taught and lived are iconic: they point beyond themselves to the One who is the Truth. Self-giving as the source of genuine human flourishing and the central moral imperative of true humanism is such a truth. This is the gospel, and the Church's raison d'être is to preach it. The Church is the Body of Christ. And thus *the* figure of this century, or any century, is Jesus Christ.

That, Pope John Paul II has insisted since his 1994 announcement of the Great Jubilee of 2000, is what the world's celebration of the turn of the millennium must recognize: that the revelation of God in the incarnate Christ is, at the same time, the revelation of true humanism.

Contributors

Romanus Cessario, O.P., is Professor of Systematic Theology at St. John's Seminary in Brighton, Massachusetts.

Jean Bethke Elshtain is the Laura Spelman Rockefeller Professor of Social and Political Ethics at the University of Chicago, and the author, most recently, of *Real Politics: At the Center of Everyday Life* (Johns Hopkins University Press).

Mary Ann Glendon is the Learned Hand Professor of Law at Harvard University.

Robert Hollander is Professor of European Literature at Princeton University and Director of the Princeton Dante Project, which can be found online at http://www.princeton.edu/~dante/pdp.html.

Alister McGrath teaches theology at Oxford University and is the author of, among other works, *John Calvin: A Life.*

David Novak holds the J. Richard and Dorothy Shiff Chair of Jewish Studies at the University of Toronto.

Edward T. Oakes, S.J., teaches in the Religious Studies Department at Regis University in Denver, Colorado.

Robert Royal is Vice President of the Ethics and Public Policy Center in Washington, D.C., and author of two new books: *The Virgin and the Dy-*

namo: Use and Abuse of Religion in the Environmental Debate (Eerdmans) and *Dante Alighieri: Divine Comedy, Divine Spirituality* (Crossroad).

GEORGE WEIGEL is the author of *Witness to Hope: The Biography of John Paul II*, recently published by HarperCollins.

ROBERT LOUIS WILKEN is the William R. Kenan, Jr. Professor of the History of Christianity at the University of Virginia.